Family Therapy and the Autism Spectrum

T0386499

The autism spectrum presents a range of communication, social, and sensory differences that are challenging for clinicians to address. *Family Therapy and the Autism Spectrum* provides a guide to conceptualizing those differences and ways to discuss them with clients and their families. Readers are provided with narrative examples illustrating the application of key concepts introduced in the text. These case examples address issues that range across the life cycle, from families with young children to ones with teens who are emerging as adults. Using the techniques learned in this book, clinicians will be able to guide families towards their positive autism narrative.

This book also features a visual framework to organize the compelling narrative of each person's autism spectrum pattern of developmental differences or brain style. Using this visual framework and the corresponding descriptive language, clinicians and families can work together to create their "autism conversations." The conversations lead to the transformative experiences of developing competencies, resiliency, and advocacy for individuals and their families. The conversations also lead individuals with spectrum differences to use empowering language, supporting their ability to develop self-advocacy and self-determination skills.

Marilyn J. Monteiro, PhD, is a licensed psychologist and expert in diagnosing autism spectrum differences in children, adolescents, and adults. She maintains a family therapy practice and thoroughly enjoys having autism conversations with individuals on the spectrum and their families.

"I have known Dr. Monteiro professionally for many years and am delighted that this book permits a wider group of people to learn from her as I am privileged to do. This book is warm, rigorous, and superb in its entirety and speaks to a crucial issue in working with families with autistic children. Both as a clinician and as the parent of a child with autism, I found this book to be immensely informative and directly useful both personally and professionally."

—Baer Ackerman, MD, *child and adolescent psychiatrist, clinical professor of psychiatry at The University of Texas Southwestern Medical School in Dallas, TX*

"Congratulations Marilyn Monteiro on yet again creating a world of wisdom in bringing together the complex world of autism, diagnosis, and intervention, and enriching us with your formidable expertise and compassion. You manage to do what most practitioners are unable to, and that is break down the stigma, barriers, and 'clinical' language that we have been conditioned to use with clients, schools, and families. Not only do you teach about the human elements of people with autism, but you provide us with the tools and most importantly, respectful language to develop trusting and respectfully mutual relationships with clients. I highly commend your new title *Family Therapy and Autism Spectrum* to practitioners, teachers, educators, parents, and siblings, and everybody who wants to learn a 'new language' and progressive framework, to work with people with autism spectrum disorder."

—Eirini Lammi, *consultant psychologist MAPS, Australian Council for Educational Research*

"Children and families with Autism Spectrum Disorder (ASD) can be one of the most difficult and exhausting populations to treat. These clients are hard to relate to and their parents often feel helpless. Dr. Monteiro concisely and clearly delineates the various aspects of ASD to make it a manageable and treatable disorder. Providing actual transcripts of sessions, she arms the practitioner with language and techniques to empower parents and children. This is a must-read for anyone working with ASD clients."

—Ray Levy, PhD, *adjunct clinical professor at SMU, clinical psychologist, author of* Try and Make Me! *and* Light Their Fire

"Rooted in her extensive knowledge and understanding of the autistic brain style, Dr. Monteiro has brilliantly written *Family Therapy and the Autism Spectrum* as a guide book for those who help individuals with autism. I was most impressed with her emphasis on the best description of each individual so as to formulate the best prescription for interaction and care."

—Peter C. Ray, MD, *behavioral & developmental pediatrician, Dallas, Texas*

"We need to change our perception of autism away from it being a disorder and disability, to having a different sensory perception, learning style, and way of thinking. Marilyn Monteiro encourages clinicians to engage in such a paradigm shift, thus improving their clinical practice. This will be appreciated by, and of practical value, to both those with autism and their families. Every current and prospective clinician needs their personal copy of her words of insight and wisdom."

—Tony Attwood, PhD, *senior consultant at The Minds and Hearts Clinic, Brisbane, Australia*

Family Therapy and the Autism Spectrum

Autism Conversations in
Narrative Practice

Marilyn J. Monteiro

Routledge
Taylor & Francis Group

NEW YORK AND LONDON

First published 2016
by Routledge
711 Third Avenue, New York, NY 10017

and by Routledge
2 Park Square, Milton Park, Abingdon, Oxon, OX14 4RN

Routledge is an imprint of the Taylor & Francis Group, an informa business

Library of Congress Cataloging-in-Publication Data
A catalog record for this book has been requested

ISBN: 978-1-138-83259-6 (hbk)
ISBN: 978-1-138-83258-9 (pbk)
ISBN: 978-1-315-73594-8 (ebk)

Typeset in Sabon
by Apex CoVantage, LLC

This book is dedicated to the many families with whom I have had the privilege of having autism conversations.

Contents

SECTION IV
Therapy Resources   **147**

Figures, Table, and Boxes

Figures

Table

Boxes

Acknowledgments

Many people provided me with the direction, encouragement, and support that led to writing this book. I began my autism conversations with families in 1983, when the special education director in the Dallas schools, Ruth Turner, invited me to join her staff and interview families as part of a developmental disabilities grant. That started me on the path of listening to families tell their stories about living with a child with autism. Lorna Wing's accessible and supportive work with families in England shaped much of my thinking at that time, as did the work of Eric Schopler and his colleagues in North Carolina. Tony Attwood and his exceptional contributions shaped my thinking as well. Tony wrote the foreword for my first book and has been a colleague who has generously supported my work and provided encouragement throughout the years. In the area of narrative therapy, Larry Campbell helped me develop clinical skills in working with the family process. He also helped me define my personal narrative.

Over the course of more than 30 years, I've evaluated thousands of children with autism spectrum differences and worked with many individuals with autism spectrum differences and their families in the therapy setting. My first book, *Autism Conversations: Evaluating Children on the Autism Spectrum Through Authentic Conversations*, and my interview protocol for identifying verbal children with autism, the Monteiro Interview Guidelines for Diagnosing Asperger's Syndrome (MIGDAS), grew out of those experiences. Jeff Manson, the president of Western Psychological Services, supported my work and published the MIGDAS and the book. My editor at Western Psychological Services, Sheri Stegall, continues to work with me as we complete the revised MIGDAS-2, with interview protocols for nonverbal and verbal children, adolescents, and adults, and their parents and teachers.

Marta Moldvai, then an associate editor at Routledge, invited me to write this book for clinicians and guided me through the initial process as the book proposal was accepted. I thoroughly enjoyed our conversations. Elizabeth Graber inherited me, and she has been a supportive, insightful, and engaged editor, guiding the manuscript through to this completed book.

My deepest love and thanks to my husband, Timothy Allen, and my son, Bennett Allen, for their love, support, and encouragement. My parents, Madelyn and Em, and my brother John, are remembered with love, as they would have been delighted to share in this chapter in the family story. In countless ways, I am grateful for the support of my extended family, friends, and colleagues.

The many individuals and families with whom I have had the privilege of having autism conversations have each, in their own way, contributed to this book. My hope is that many families will benefit when clinicians apply these autism conversations to their narrative practices.

Author's Note

The narrative examples throughout this book represent composites of children, adolescents, young adults, and their families with whom I have worked over the past 30 years. They are based on my cumulative experience and are used to help the reader experience therapy conversations while protecting the confidentiality of individuals.

An Initial Conversation

Every individual with autism spectrum differences has a story to tell. The conversations in this book were written to help you gain an appreciation of the rich, varied, and multilayered dimensions the autism spectrum brain style brings to the lives of children, adolescents, young adults, and their families. As a clinician, you play a key role in supporting individuals and their families as they discover their unique and singular autism narrative.

This is a book for clinicians working with individuals and their families in the therapy context. As you read this book, you can expect to gain a comprehensive understanding of the autism spectrum, along with practical strategies to apply in your clinical practice. You will become better able to recognize the autism brain style in children, adolescents, and young adults, and to support the development of empowered narratives for individuals and their families. Readers who are interested in pursuing specific expertise in autism evaluations are referred to my first book: *Autism Conversations: Evaluating Children on the Autism Spectrum Through Authentic Conversations.*

The first section of this book introduces you to a way to think—and talk—about the autism spectrum brain style in a way that naturally leads to the unfolding of an individualized narrative for children, adolescents, young adults, and their families. The visual framework described in this book has formed the foundation of my autism conversations over the past 30 years. It provides the starting point in the therapy conversation as you guide each child, adolescent, and young adult—and each of their families—through the process of developing their unique and singular stories.

The visual framework described in this book shifts the conversation away from the label, or diagnosis, and centers the conversation on the individual. Within the conversation, the autism spectrum brain style differences are identified and described, but the focus is firmly set on the individual experience rather than the diagnostic label. The framework presented in this book provides you with a framework to guide your autism conversations in your narrative practice.

From that beginning, in the second section of this book you will accompany families as they are guided through four key narrative shifts: from powerless to capable, from dysregulated to controlled, from prompt-dependence to autonomy, and from disorder to style. Narrative therapy techniques are a part of each family's autism conversation with the clinician. The specific tools are both demonstrated in the narratives and described for the reader.

The third section of this book takes you through four life-cycle stages: young children, children, adolescents, and young adults. Therapy conversations at each stage of development feature key narrative therapy supports that help individuals with autism spectrum differences and their families gain understanding, skills, emotional balance, and a positive narrative thread.

The fourth section of this book provides the reader with therapy resources under three general categories: organizational supports, regulation supports, and social narrative supports.

I am delighted that we will be sharing these autism conversations in narrative practice as you read this book. Let's start with our conversation about a practical framework for clinicians.

Section I
The Visual Framework

1 A Practical Framework for Clinicians

The Visual Framework

- The framework gives clinicians an accessible way to think—and talk—about autism spectrum differences with individuals and their families.
- The descriptive triangle graphic provides a visual starting point for the autism conversation.
- The framework introduces the narrative of brain style differences.

Descriptive Language Replaces the Diagnostic Label

- Brain style strengths and differences are described within the context of the visual framework.
- Descriptive language naturally leads to a conversation about what supports and strategies are the best fit for the individual's brain style differences.
- Descriptive language and the visual framework support emotional resiliency.

Singular Presentation of the Global Criteria

- Starts with a working knowledge of the global criteria;
- Unfolds as the clinician structures the "autism conversation" with individuals and their families;
- Produces an individual Brain Style Profile.

Autism stories have become an integral part of the general culture across the globe.

With only a few degrees of separation, every person knows—or knows of—a child, adolescent, or adult with autism. For most clinicians, the term "autism" conjures up a certain combination of behaviors while the term "Asperger's Syndrome" evokes quite a different set of traits. Expectations about what characteristics embody autism in an individual are often limited by direct experience. As you read the therapy conversations in this book, you can expect to expand your conceptualization and understanding of how autism spectrum differences look and present themselves in individuals across ability levels and the life cycle.

Especially with individuals who fall on the milder, high-functioning end of the spectrum, it can be challenging for clinicians to recognize key autism differences in the therapy setting. Females with autism spectrum differences, for example, are more likely to be diagnosed as having clinical depression or generalized anxiety conditions while their underlying autism spectrum differences remain unidentified or unexplored.[1] Males may initially be perceived as having a behavior disorder when in actuality their patterns of reactive and disruptive behaviors are a direct function of their underlying autism spectrum differences.[2] Learning to recognize the autism spectrum differences profile in children, adolescents, and young adults is an essential part of providing effective therapy and interventions in the clinical setting.

Since May of 2013 when the American Psychiatric Association published the fifth edition of the *Diagnostic and Statistical Manual of Mental Disorders* (DSM-5) the diagnostic terminology has focused on a single term: Autism Spectrum Disorder.[3] Previously, individuals with autism spectrum differences were identified as having one of three distinct conditions: Autistic Disorder; Asperger's Syndrome; or Pervasive Developmental Disorder, Not Otherwise Specified. In practice, it was often difficult to place individuals neatly into one of those three distinct diagnostic categories, as the neurobiological behavioral differences that characterize autism are complex, often nuanced, and fall on a spectrum or continuum.

The DSM-5 identifies two distinct domains as the core of the Autism Spectrum Disorder criteria: *social communication deficits* and *restricted, repetitive behaviors*. Individuals who meet the core criteria are then assigned a severity level for each of the two core domains. The severity levels range from Level 1 (*requires support*) to Level 3 (*requires very substantial support*). Additional components of the DSM-5 diagnostic criteria include an indication the individual displays some degree of clinical impairment in current functioning, a presence of the behaviors during early childhood even though full presentation may not become apparent until a later developmental period, and behaviors that cannot be better explained by the presence of an intellectual impairment.

Autism Spectrum Disorder is considered to be a neuro-biological developmental disorder that is diagnosed based on a clinical assessment of symptoms and diagnostic tests. The diagnosis is based on the preponderance of data and evidence collected through observations, interviews,[4] autism-specific assessment rating scales,[5] and autism-specific evaluation instruments.[6] In other words, identifying individuals who are functioning with autism spectrum differences is a complex and multifaceted process that requires clinicians to collect and interpret multiple sources of information.[7]

As clinicians, of course it is important to be thoroughly familiar with the current diagnostic criteria. However, knowledge of the criteria does not lead to a natural way to discuss diagnostic observations with patients. It does not help us talk with individuals and families in terms that help them construct and tell their singular story. The language of the diagnostic criteria is negative by design, as it emphasizes deficits and severity levels. This is important when distinguishing between a condition and the presence of a few behavioral characteristics, but it does not prepare clinicians to discuss the diagnosis with individuals and their families.

The Visual Framework

"Change the story and you change the life."

Sylvie, a slender 20-year-old young woman, emphasized her two-part statement by extending her right hand and then her left. That said, she dropped her hands into her lap.

"When I was little, they told me I was anxious and depressed. Then, when I was older, they told me I was *severely* anxious and *severely* depressed. So I was defective. There was something wrong with me." Sylvie frowned as she recalled these labels. She raised her eyebrows and repeated her precise hand gestures as she continued.

"But now, since we've been coming here, I have a way to understand why I was so anxious all the time. I understand my brain style. I just see things differently."

She paused for a moment, reflecting. She smiled as she continued.

"And so do a lot of other people I know."

The language we use shapes the way individuals and families create their unique stories. Where do we begin? How do we think about the individual's autism spectrum profile? How do we talk about that profile with the individual and his or her family?

In my conversations with individuals and their families, I use a visual framework that emphasizes describing a pattern of differences that fit the individual. The visual framework lays out an accessible way to think—and talk—about autism spectrum differences. Using this framework and the accompanying graphic of the descriptive triangle will help you recognize the scope of autism spectrum differences in the clinical setting. Think of the framework and the descriptive triangle as a visual starting point for the family's narrative about their child's developmental differences. Familiarizing yourself with this framework prepares you to support individuals and families in their understanding of exactly what the term "autism spectrum" means and how it applies to their singular situation.

The visual nature of this framework gives you a way to introduce the narrative of brain style differences. The conversation shifts from the identification of a disorder or a deficit level of functioning to the identification of brain style differences. By definition, differences come with areas of strength or ability. The language of differences shifts the conversation into emotionally neutral territory, as the diagnosis of autism is externalized into a framework that focuses on describing how the individual's brain organizes language, social, emotional, and sensory information. You can have a dialogue with families where curiosity about the individual's differences becomes the focus. Questions focus on finding ways to describe and understand the world from the perspective of the individual with brain style differences. What is the perspective of the child? What is the child's communication style? As you help families construct the child's individualized Brain Style Profile, the conversation leads to a discussion of creative ways to manage differences.

When I work with young children and their families, I often draw the following graphic of the descriptive triangle as we talk about the child's patterns of *differences in development* in three key areas:

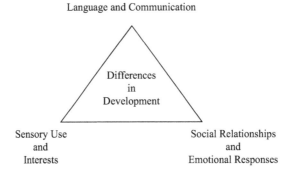

Figure 1.1 Descriptive Triangle Differences in Development. Reprinted with permission.[8]

The center of the triangle contains the term *differences in development* instead of the words "autism spectrum disorder." This wording is important, as it takes the emphasis off of the label and places it on a description of the process. The question shifts from asking if the child has a form of autism to becoming curious about whether or not the child shows a pattern of differences in his or her development.

When working with older children, adolescents, and young adults, the language changes as follows:

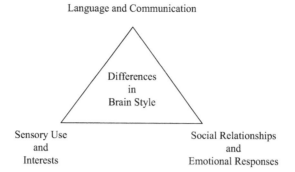

Language and Communication

Differences
in
Brain Style

Sensory Use
and
Interests

Social Relationships
and
Emotional Responses

Figure 1.2 Descriptive Triangle Differences in Brain Style

The term *differences in brain style* introduces a fundamentally positive narrative. Everyone has a brain style. Differences in development
or brain style associated with the autism spectrum come with identifi-
able areas of strength as well as areas of distinctive gaps between how
neuro-typical and neuro-atypical individuals manage social, communication, and sensory demands. The descriptive triangle prompts you to
develop an individualized behavioral profile that emphasizes areas of
strength and areas of distinctive differences in each of the three key areas
for the children, adolescents, and young adults you see who have autism
spectrum differences.

You'll notice that the descriptive triangle graphics in the first two figures do not contain the words "autism spectrum disorder." Starting the
autism conversation by visually laying out the pattern of differences in
development or brain style emphasizes the individual narrative. The story
centers on laying out the individual's pattern or style of functioning in the
world. The story you are building is not the story of autism. The visual
framework provides the structure to build the story of the individual.

When you are working with families who have already received a formal diagnosis for their child, the visual framework and the accompanying
descriptive language helps families make sense out of their child's diagnosis. If you are working with a family for whom a formal diagnosis has not
yet been given to their child, the visual framework provides you with a
way to describe the individual. This lays the groundwork for you to make
a referral for the family to pursue a comprehensive autism evaluation.

Although the DSM-5 configures autism spectrum domains into two
areas (*social communication deficits* and *restricted, repetitive behaviors*),
the visual framework addresses three distinct areas: *language and communication, social relationships and emotional responses*, and *sensory
use and interests*. The division of the first domain (*social communication
deficits*) into two (*language and communication* and *social relationships
and emotional responses*) allows for a more detailed description of the
individual's behavioral profile, as it separates out communication and

social relationships, while addressing emotional responses in the context of social relationships.

The third area, *sensory use and interests*, addresses *restricted, repetitive behaviors* while changing the language to promote an understanding of the individual's sensory-driven behaviors in a positive and adaptive context. Discussing an individual's behavior patterns as *restricted and repetitive* labels the behavior as negative and by definition becomes an undesirable attribute.

Discussing an individual's *areas of preferred interest* and *sensory use* (what types of sensory experiences they seek out to regulate and organize and what types of sensory experiences create distress and disorganization) shifts the conversation by externalizing their preferences and by introducing the use of positive language. For example, instead of thinking of the child as "obsessing" or "perseverating" on a topic or activity, the visual framework language reframes this as "areas of preferred interest," and the child as having a "high threshold for systematic routines." This externalization promotes a discussion of the form and function of the individual's interests and routines, promoting solution-based outcomes. It empowers the individual and his or her family to appreciate the perspective of the individual with autism spectrum differences.

The visual framework, then, leads us to think about individuals with Autism Spectrum Disorder in a distinctive way. Individuals with Autism Spectrum Disorder display a pattern of differences in their development, or style, that affects the way they use language and communicate with others; how they understand and participate in social relationships; the way in which they understand, manage, and regulate emotions; and how they respond to and manage sensory input and preferred areas of interest.

Individuals with autism spectrum differences organize their behavior and worldview primarily around the area of *sensory use and interests*, in contrast with individuals who do not have this pattern of differences. Their natural entry point for organizing their behavior and managing in the world is the entry point of *sensory use and interests*, not communication or social relationships and emotional responses. Even highly verbal individuals with autism spectrum differences show a drive to communicate information about their topics of interests while struggling to participate in conversations with others that revolve around social topics and require reciprocity, flexibility, and extension of topics. The complex behavioral patterns that are part of communication, social exchanges, and emotional regulation are typically areas that are sources of stress and create challenges for individuals with autism spectrum differences. At the same time, they find it calming and regulating when they are able to engage in sensory-seeking routines or pursue their areas of preferred interest.

It is important to note that many individuals with autism spectrum differences have a social drive and seek out relationships with others.

The difficulties arise for them when they struggle with the gap between their desire for social relationships and their ability to interpret, manage, and apply social cues. In contrast, children, adolescents, and young adults who do not function with the pattern of differences that comprise the autism spectrum may have distinctive areas of interest and sensory preferences but they organize in the world primarily through communication with others, and through shared social and emotional relationships.

Going back to the descriptive triangle, you can visually emphasize the organizing role that the area of sensory use and interests plays by drawing a circle around those words:

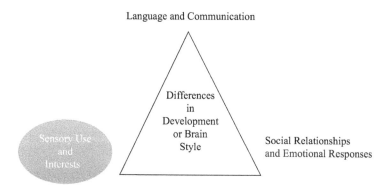

Figure 1.3 Descriptive Triangle and the Sensory Entry Point

This graphic depiction of the sensory entry point can readily lead to a discussion of the form and function of the individual's sensory-seeking routines and areas of preferred interest. An interest in building with Legos, for example, can be discussed as an activity that requires three-dimensional thinking and visual organization while giving the individual a break from managing incoming language and social demands. The form is three-dimensional and visual, while the function is organizational, leading to a regulation of emotions and a reprieve from the stress inherent in managing the complexities that are a part of social and language interactions. Instead of discussing the child's interest in building with Legos as restrictive and repetitive, the narrative shifts to a discussion of the child's strengths as a "three-dimensional thinker." This reframe can then be used to guide individuals and families to build effective strategies and solutions to improve communication and social and emotional skill sets.

Now let's combine the visual framework with the DSM-5 core domain areas and levels of support. They can be interconnected as follows:

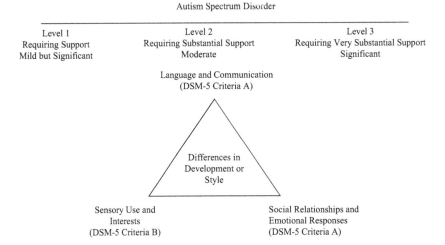

Figure 1.4 Descriptive Triangle and DSM-5 Core Domains

Now we have a visual framework that lays out the key differences in development or brain style, with the added dimension of addressing the following essential question: How much is the individual's pattern of brain style differences getting in the way of his or her ability to function? The DSM-5 criteria addresses this question with the assignment of levels of support. In the visual framework, the language of degree is used, ranging from *mild but significant* to *significant*. The word "significant" is used rather than the word "severe," in keeping with the descriptive rather than labeling terminology.

Replacing Diagnostic Labels with Descriptive Language

Within the context of the visual framework, clinicians benefit from being able to replace diagnostic labels with descriptive language. The use of descriptive language shapes the narrative between the clinician and the family. The conversation moves away from the use of diagnostic terms and towards nuanced observations that are representative of the individual with autism spectrum differences. Brain style strengths and differences are described, leading to a discussion of ways in which the individual's areas of strength can be linked to practical support strategies. The therapeutic conversations focus on shaping an understanding of how autism spectrum differences affect perceptions and behavior while conveying respect for the individual's unique worldview. Once the descriptive narrative is adopted as an integral part of the therapeutic conversation, the development of emotional resiliency and creative alternatives to unsuccessful behavior patterns are a natural outgrowth.

So how does one go about describing autism spectrum differences in children, adolescents, and young adults in a way that is organized, comprehensive, and accessible to individuals and their families? Using the visual framework, the key differences in development or style in the areas of language and communication, social relationships and emotional responses, and sensory use and interests can be summarized descriptively in a succinct format. Table 1.1 provides an organized way to think about and recognize the distinctive pattern of differences that describe the presentation of the autism spectrum differences profile. The division of the spectrum into the three levels of support across the three key areas of differences is designed to help clinicians recognize the range of autism spectrum differences in a comprehensive way. Familiarizing yourself with the descriptive language laid out in Table 1.1 will help you apply that language when you guide families through the process of building Brain Style Profiles.

Here are a few examples highlighting the descriptive language from Table 1.1.

In the area of language and communication, individuals with mild but significant differences have well-developed language but use their language in distinctively different ways than their neuro-typical counterparts. They usually have developed one or more areas of passionate interest, and conversations with others frequently focus on conveying facts and details about those preferred topics. They engage in a pattern of "sensory-driven" speech; that is, they appear to repeat details primarily for their own benefit rather than conveying information in a shared, reciprocal, social exchange. Their ability to organize and use language markedly declines when they respond to conversational topics selected by others, during socially driven conversations, and when discussing emotions. They may use some nonverbal communications functions, such as eye contact and gestures, but these are often not well integrated and they display inconsistency in their use and interpretation of social communication cues.

In contrast, individuals with significant differences in their use of language and communication may be functionally nonverbal, meaning they use only a few words for communication purposes. When verbal skills are present, the individual organizes his or her use of language around labeling objects and qualities of objects, and around the use of scripted language from areas of his or her preferred interests. As a result of this organization of language around labeling, their expressive language is more developed than receptive language in everyday situations. Receptive language is most organized when verbal requests are paired with visual contextual cues; in other words, when they are shown what is requested in addition to being verbally asked. Nonverbal communication functions such as eye gaze, gestures, and joint attention are rarely used.

Table 1.1 DSM-5 Autism Spectrum Disorder Levels of Support: Using the Autism Conversations Descriptive Triangle to Individualize the Diagnosis

	Level 1: Requiring Support Mild but Significant	Level 2: Requiring Substantial Support Moderate	Level 3: Requiring Very Substantial Support Significant
DSM-5 Criteria A Language and Communication: (DSM-5 Social Communication)	Language skills well developed Usually has developed one or more areas of passionate interest Conversation with others focuses on conveying facts and details about preferred topics Sensory-driven speech (the person appears to repeat details primarily for his or her benefit rather than sharing information for social interaction) Ability to organize and use language diminishes when responding to others in social situations, and when discussing emotions Some demonstrated use of nonverbal communication functions but inconsistent in the ability to interpret and use common cues	Language skills typically less developed than in individuals at Level 1 Use of language is prompt-dependent on adults May have developed one or more areas of passionate interest but has difficulty communicating details with others May initiate conversation but notable difficulties with reciprocal conversation Inflexible and limited in ability to participate in an extended conversation Use of repetitive questions and phrases is commonly seen Use of nonverbal communication cues inconsistent and infrequent	May be functionally nonverbal Rarely uses nonverbal communication functions (eye gaze, gestures, joint attention) When verbal skills are present: Vocabulary is organized around labeling Use of language is rote and self-directed with frequent use of scripted language Comments are rarely directed towards a listener Expressive language more developed than receptive language in everyday situations Receptive language most organized when verbal requests are paired with visual contextual cues

DSM-5 Criteria A Social Relationships and Emotional Responses: (DSM-5 Social Communication)	Usually initiates and extends social exchanges but does so on his or her own agenda Most comfortable with adults or younger children even though a desire for peer relationships is generally present Peer relationships are often a source of anxiety and are experienced as perplexing May have difficulty regulating emotional states as evidenced by inflexibility, explosive outbursts, behavior escalation	Prompt-dependent on others to structure social exchanges and may be able to initiate and extend as long as structure is present Lacks flexibility in play as a child and in work or social routines as an adult May become anxious and agitated during loosely structured language and social interactions Access to language significantly decreases as emotional distress increases	Becomes anxious with social exchanges and does not generally initiate or sustain social interactions Tends to remove self from social exchanges Most comfortable with others when sharing sensory interests and when limited language is used Easily distressed by unexpected changes in routine When agitated or distressed responds best when language use is limited and visual prompts are provided
DSM-5 Criteria B Sensory Use and Interests: (DSM-5 Restricted Interests and Repetitive Behaviors)	Has developed one or more areas of passionate interests that may be age-appropriate in content but unusual in the individual's focus and intense interest Sensory-driven quality to the narrative when sharing information with others about preferred topics Sensory triggers (noises, textures, changes in routine, perceived "unfairness") lead to decrease in access to language and the individual reverts to the use of inflexible, agitated, immature, or unusual behaviors Unusual body movements are subtle but repetitive	Displays some drive to establish sensory-driven play or pursuit of interests but can be redirected by others During social play as a child and in social situations as an adult, tends to create and follow rigid and inflexible play or conversational routines Infrequent display of unusual body movements and mannerisms may be noted during times of stress or during solitary pursuit of interests	Tends to focus intently on the sensory aspects of materials Seeks out manipulative materials with visual and tactile features Creates repetitive sensory routines as a means to self-regulate anxiety Frequently displays distinctive unusual body movements and mannerisms

In the area of social relationships and emotional responses, individuals with mild but significant differences usually initiate and extend social exchanges but do so by following their own agenda. This means they seek out social connection with others but follow their own idea of how that interaction should unfold. This leads to a pattern of one-sided interactions, with the individual initiating the exchange without a corresponding ability to look for and respond to social cues from a conversational partner. There is oftentimes a pattern of the individual seeking out relationships with older and younger people while avoiding or struggling to successfully function in relationships with same-age peers. Individuals with mild but significant autism spectrum social differences display a genuine enjoyment in sharing areas of interest with same-age peers, paired with puzzlement over why peer friendships are so difficult to navigate. Peer relationships are a source of anxiety and may be perceived as perplexing and as a source of frustration. This can lead to feelings of being defective and to a sense of marginalization. They may display difficulty regulating and managing agitation and intense emotional states, as evidenced by explosive outbursts, behavior escalation, and inflexibility.

Individuals with moderate differences in the area of social relationships and emotional responses enjoy social relationships to some degree and in some situations but are prompt-dependent on others to structure social exchanges and to keep them going. These individuals may be able to initiate and extend as long as the prompts and structure are provided but have difficulty engaging in social exchanges in the absence of predictable structure and prompts. They may become anxious or agitated in loosely structured social and language interactions and as a result may engage in immature or unusual behaviors, or withdraw from the social setting. Their ability to access their language skills significantly decreases as their emotional distress increases.

In the area of sensory use and interests, individuals with mild but significant differences have usually developed one or more areas of passionate interest, and these interests may change over time. The interests may be age-appropriate in their content but unusual in the individual's focus and intensity. Sensory sensitivity triggers, such as noises, textures, changes in routine, and perceived unfairness, lead to a decreased access to language skills. As a result, the high-functioning individual unexpectedly reverts to the use of inflexible, agitated, immature, or unusual behaviors when sensory sensitivities are triggered. The individual usually displays a pattern of unusual body movements or mannerisms but these are typically subtle and not apparent in all settings.

Individuals with significant differences in the area of sensory use and interests tend to focus intently on the sensory aspects of materials and their surroundings. They oftentimes seek out materials with specific visual and tactile properties and manipulate them in systematic ways.

They create repetitive sensory routines as a means to self-regulate anxiety and to block out incoming language and social demands. It is common to see a pattern of distinctive and unusual body movements and mannerisms, and their use of these routines increases both in times of distress and when the individual is engaged in pleasurable sensory-seeking routines.

Singular Presentation of the Global Criteria

Families benefit from working with clinicians who can describe the family member with autism spectrum differences in accessible, individualized language while de-emphasizing the autism diagnostic terminology. This requires the clinician to apply the global criteria to each singular presentation. Exactly what does this process entail? How does a clinician go about recognizing and discussing an individual's autism spectrum behavioral profile?

The process starts with a working knowledge of the global criteria, both in terms of the current diagnostic parameters and the ability to organize the understanding of the global criteria into the visual framework with the corresponding descriptive language.

Clinicians must also learn to recognize the behavior patterns associated with autism spectrum differences in their clinical practice. This requires the ability to draw out the behavior sample in conversation with individuals and their families in the therapy setting. How does one elicit the behavior sample to determine whether or not a pattern of autism spectrum differences is part of the therapeutic conversation? This is done through a process I call having an *autism conversation*. Autism conversations begin with an entry point of talking about the individual's areas of preferred interest in a dynamic and interactive way. Most individuals with autism spectrum differences display a notable increase in alertness and engagement when their topics of preferred interest are introduced and pursued in conversation with another person. With adolescents and young adults who have well-developed verbal skills, the autism conversation entry point is typically introduced when the clinician expresses an interest in—and knowledge of—the individual's area of preferred interest. Starting the session with questions about the individual's preferred activities often provides a natural entry point into the autism conversation.

At the start of my initial session with Tyler, a 15-year-old adolescent with an angular build and an intense, serious demeanor, I asked him what types of things he enjoys doing when he is not studying or in school.

"Anything that has to do with movies. Right now I am particularly interested in movies that feature Don Knotts. He was a legendary television character actor who went on to star in a number of comedies in the 1960s and 70s. Of course his actual name was Jesse Donald but he was always known as Don Knotts."

"Which Don Knotts comedy would you consider to be his best work?"

"Well, of course most people would say 'The Incredible Mr. Limpett.' It's considered to be a classic, partly because it was a movie where Don Knotts played a character who was animated in some scenes but live action in others. It was directed by Arthur Lubin who also directed the classic TV series 'Mr. Ed.' But my personal favorite is 'The Ghost and Mr. Chicken.' It was directed by Alan Rafkin. They worked together when Don Knotts played the classic character of Deputy Barney Fife in the 'Andy Griffith Show.' Alan Rafkin directed a number of episodes. Of course, Don Knotts always played characters that were meek and mild mannered but who also became easily flustered."

"He was quite an actor. When he was Deputy Barney Fife, wasn't he always making 'citizen's arrests'?"

"Well, actually, Gomer was the one who performed the citizen's arrest when Barney Fife made an illegal u-turn. Barney Fife was a deputy so he made actual arrests."

"Of course. Wasn't Don Knotts also in a movie about an astronaut?"

"Oh, yes, that was another classic. 'The Reluctant Astronaut' was released by Universal in 1967. Don Knotts plays the character of Ron Fleming, a mild mannered operator of kiddie rides who is afraid of heights. His father signs him up for the astronaut program. Arthur O'Connell played his father."

"Tyler, you know a lot of facts about Don Knotts and also about other actors and directors. Tell me how you keep all of the details organized."

"Well, I like to read the credits to all of the movies I watch, and also I read background information on IMDB. That's the Internet Movie Data Base. Then I make my lists. Currently my movie list includes my favorite movies."

"So you organize and remember the information through reading and making lists. How many movies are on your favorites list?"

"Well, right now the list contains 1,000 movies. Every time I think about taking a movie off the list, I review the details and find a reason the movie continues to belong there."

What specifically characterizes this example as an "autism conversation?" Many individuals respond to questions about their areas of interest. However, in a therapy context, individuals who have autism spectrum differences are not only responsive to prompts to discuss areas of preferred interest but also display a pattern of continuing with the topic for an extended period of time and in an increasingly detailed and one-sided way. As the clinician participates in such conversations, they are able to gain a sample of the form and function of the individual's sensory-based interest. As the conversation progresses, for example, does it become increasingly more difficult to interrupt the individual's narrative? Does that narrative focus on conveying facts and details to the exclusion of social information? Does the individual frequently correct comments made by the conversational partner and redirect the conversation by using recurrent phrases such as "well, actually" or "as a matter of fact"? Is there a sense that as a conversational partner you are working hard to stay in the conversation? Are attempts to shift the conversation to social and emotional content met with a notable decrease in verbal output, both in terms of the quantity and quality of language used? Neuro-typical individuals who are invited by clinicians to share information about their interests do so in a shared reciprocal exchange, with a sense of back-and-forth conversation. They typically provide verbal and nonverbal communication cues that signal an interest in shifting the therapy dialogue to conversational topics that are relevant to the therapy context.

The autism conversation entry point connects the clinician with the adolescent or young adult in a powerful and genuine way. In Tyler's case, forging a bond through the detailed conversation about his area of passionate interest helped him relax and communicate at length. It provided me with valuable information about the form and function of Tyler's sensory-driven interest. The form was visual and was driven by the structure of organizing and categorizing information. Tyler's interest in information about movies served the function of organizing his language and allowed him to participate in a conversation that was predictable as long as he stayed in charge of the topic. Establishing our connection through Tyler's interest in movies was the first step in understanding his worldview and helping him shape his overall narrative as the therapy process moved forward.

The autism conversation entry point with children who come into the therapy setting with their parents usually includes manipulative materials that contain interesting sensory properties. High-functioning individuals with autism spectrum differences do not always display notable behavioral differences in all situations or settings, as they have mastered the necessary skills to function in an adaptive way. In the therapy setting, individuals with autism spectrum differences oftentimes respond to the language-dense interactions with low energy output and limited social engagement. Many high-functioning children, adolescents, and young adults have learned to follow the prompts provided by the adult who is structuring the interaction. As a result, in the therapy setting, many times the individual may not initiate a conversation about preferred topics or areas of interest unless the adult in charge introduces a topic, either through verbal conversation or a combination of conversation and the presentation of tangible objects for the individual to look at and manipulate. It can be challenging to engage the individual with autism spectrum differences in a productive therapy dialogue. With children, starting with the sensory entry point leads to a powerful connection with the clinician during the initial session, providing a starting point to develop individualized strategies and interventions.

Eliot, a seven-year-old boy, came to his initial session with his mother, Ruth. Ruth and I spoke over the phone prior to our meeting and she told me her main areas of concern regarding her son. She also completed a detailed parent interview containing questions designed to encourage her to tell stories about Eliot that included information about his favorite activities and the qualities she liked most about him. I learned that Eliot had an intense interest in building with Legos, and collecting matchbox cars. Prior to their session, I set out a several sets of magnets that fit together to construct various geometric shapes, along with their accompanying instruction books. When I went to greet Eliot and his mother, Eliot was standing in front of the door with an expectant look on his face. I noticed that he was wearing a small cross-body bag about the size and shape of a case for a pair of binoculars. The sides bulged slightly with the contents. As I said hello he strode past me and entered the room, where he quickly took in the presence of the magnets. Eliot planted his feet on the floor and in one fluid move he lowered himself to balance on his haunches in front of the chair where the magnets were arranged. His back was towards me as I sat down next to him. His mother prompted Eliot to say hello, which he did without turning around, as his attention was intently focused on the magnets. He was already deeply engaged in the process of handling the magnets and configuring them in various ways.

"The red magnets can fit together to make a ball, like the one on the cover of the book," I commented.

"The Ball of Whacks!" Eliot read the title of the book. When he spoke he used an exclamatory tone of voice, and he spoke in a somewhat loud and formal way. "And this one is called the X-Ball, and the pieces have a slightly different shape. In fact, you could say the Ball of Whacks forms a solid ball and the X-Ball does not!"

"Yes, and you could also say that maybe the Ball of Whacks can fit inside the X-Ball!" I mirrored the enthusiastic way Eliot spoke and followed his conversational lead. We were beginning our autism conversation. We continued to talk about the various properties of the magnets while Eliot continued to configure them in various ways. After a few minutes of conversation directed towards the back of Eliot's head, I asked a question to direct his attention to the contents of his cross-body bag.

"Eliot, I like the bag you brought with you. Would you show me what's inside?"

"Of course! I carry this bag with me wherever I go." He patted the front of the bag that was positioned across his body. As he unsnapped the closure and lifted the flap he swiveled his body so his profile was directly in front of me.

"Your mom told me that you like to collect cars."

Eliot glanced quickly in my direction for the first time. "As a matter of fact I do!" He began removing the miniature vehicles, carefully examining the details of each one before placing them in a line in front of him.

He held a tractor-trailer truck up and faintly waved in in my general direction. "This one is actually Optimus Prime."

"The leader of the Transformers!" I exclaimed.

"Well, he's actually the leader of the Autobots, not the Decepticons. Their leader is Megatron."

"That's right. Does your Optimus Prime truck transform?"

"No, but he does have Optimus painted on this side." Eliot turned the truck over and thrust it in my general direction.

I reached out my hand. "Oh, can I see?" Eliot handed the truck to me and I looked at the painted figure. "That's a good picture of Optimus. I can see why he's the leader of the good guys."

Eliot had already begun examining another vehicle while I looked at the truck and made my comments. He picked up a yellow car and held it up in front of his line of vision. "And this is Bumblebee after he became a new Camaro. Not when he was the old Camaro."

Having the magnets set up in the session room prior to his arrival facilitated this "autism conversation" with Eliot. From his perspective, the presence of the visually interesting toys was a perfect fit with his sensory-based worldview. Commenting on the properties of the magnets at the start of our verbal conversation sent an additional signal that we would be following his interests instead of setting a more social agenda. Mirroring his way of speaking, and prompting Eliot to share the contents of his cross-body bag, also fit well with his autism spectrum worldview, as he clearly responded to me as if I was an extension of his perspective.

Adapting the environment and the conversation to fit the agenda of the child provides important information. Children who do not have the differences that come with the autism spectrum worldview quickly display a wide range of social, emotional, and communication behavior patterns that include consistently referencing the adult. The contrast between neuro-typical children and children with autism spectrum differences is striking when the therapy session begins with the sensory entry point. In Eliot's case, he had difficulty integrating social cues into his play and dialogue. He used references that were clear to him but included details that made it difficult for his conversational partner to follow along.

Having his mother complete a detailed interview prior to the initial session helped me prepare for Eliot's current areas of preferred interest so I could understand and comment on his detailed points of reference. Eliot's alertness, focus, and engagement with the materials and by extension, with the conversation with a new adult in a new setting, were elicited in a clear way that provided a pleasant experience for him and his mother. This positive first meeting provided the entry point for developing Eliot's individualized autism narrative.

Now let's explore how to build on the autism conversation to guide individuals and their families to develop an empowered narrative.

Notes

1   Attwood, Tony (2012). "Girls with Asperger's Syndrome: Early Diagnosis Is Critical." *Autism Asperger's Digest*, July/August 2012.
2   Baron-Cohen, Simon (2004). *The Essential Differences: Male and Female Brains and the Truth About Autism*. New York, NY: Basic Books.
3   American Psychiatric Association (2013). *Diagnostic and Statistical Manual of Mental Disorders, Fifth Edition*. Washington, DC: American Psychiatric Publishing.
4   Monteiro, Marilyn J. (2008). *Monteiro Interview Guidelines for Diagnosing Asperger's Syndrome (MIGDAS) Parent and Teacher Interview*. Los Angeles, CA: Western Psychological Services.
5   Constantino, John M., and Gruber, Christian P. (2012). *Social Responsiveness Scale, Second Edition (SRS-2)*. Los Angeles, CA: Western Psychological Services; Goldstein, Sam, and Naglieri, Jack (2009). *Autism Spectrum Rating Scales (ASRS)*. New York, NY: MHS Publishers; Schopler, Eric, Van Bourgondien, Mary E., Wellman, Glenna Janette, and Love, Steven R. (2010). *Childhood Autism Rating Scale, 2nd Edition*. Los Angeles, CA: Western Psychological Publishing.
6   Lord, Catherine (1999). *Autism Diagnostic Observation Schedule 2 (ADOS-2)*. Los Angeles, CA: Western Psychological Publishing; Monteiro, Marilyn J. (2008). *Monteiro Interview Guidelines for Diagnosing Asperger's Syndrome (MIGDAS) Diagnostic Student Interview*. Los Angeles, CA: Western Psychological Services.
7   Klin, Ami, Saulnier, Celine, Tsatsanis, Katherine, and Volkmar, Fred R. (2005). *Clinical Evaluations in Autism Spectrum Disorders: Psychological Assessment within a Transdisciplinary Framework* in Volkmar, Fred R., Paul, Rhea, Klin, Ami, and Cohen, Donald *Handbook of Autism and Pervasive Developmental Disorders, Volume One, Third Edition*. Hoboken, NJ: John Wiley & Sons.
8   Monteiro, Marilyn J. (2010). *Autism Conversations: Evaluating Children on the Autism Spectrum Through Authentic Conversations*. Los Angeles, CA: Western Psychological Services.

2 Narrative Therapy Practices and the Autism Spectrum

The Global Diagnostic Label

- Opens the gateway to the vast world of autism spectrum culture.
- Introduces a family narrative that radically shifts the prior story.
- Increases family stress in the face of determining how entering the world of autism spectrum differences will fit into the existing family story.

Moving Beyond the Global Diagnostic Label with the Singular Presentation Narrative

- Encourages the resetting of individual and family stories using individual style as the organizing framework.
- Enables family members to construct individual narratives that are multilayered, complex, and transformative.
- Expands the conversation to allow for an exploration of the strategies and supports that best fit the style of the individual and the family system.

Identifying the Dominant Story

- Starting the autism conversation with parents.
- Using visual supports and creating documents.
- Four key narrative shifts.

The Global Diagnostic Label and the Autism Spectrum Narrative

A diagnosis of Autism Spectrum Disorder introduces a strong story line for individuals and their families. Each family approaches this crossroad in their unfolding narrative of family life in a unique, diverse, and multi-layered way. There are as many ways to incorporate the autism narrative into the ongoing family story as can be imagined. The way in which individuals and families make sense out of a child, adolescent, or young adult autism spectrum diagnosis cannot be readily anticipated or summarized through the lens of others. Each family goes through an incomparable process of constructing their specific autism spectrum story. And yet all families share a common task: making sense of the diagnosis and config-uring the identification of the family member's autism spectrum differ-ences into the existing story lines.

The diagnosis is initially often explained to parents in a way that embodies the story of an existing problem, or problem behaviors, or developmental disability. The diagnostic label—Autism Spectrum Disorder—immediately thrusts parents into the story line of naming the problem. The entire family is transported to a narrative that hems them in with restrictive boundaries and limitations.[1] There is a strong pull towards internalizing the diagnosis as a state of "otherness," separating their experiences from those of families perceived as typical or conform-ing to the conventions of standard family life in the community. In fact, long before parents receive a formal autism spectrum diagnosis for their child, they have already begun to experience their family life as existing in a state of "otherness." Some families experience relief when their child, adolescent, or even adult family member receives a diagnosis of Autism Spectrum Disorder. The diagnosis helps explain puzzling behaviors and why the child, adolescent, or adult has struggled so mightily in response to demands to "go with the flow" in school, home, social, and work settings.

Even when the diagnosis brings a sense of relief, the label itself encour-ages the identification of a problem that lies within the individual. Parents who receive the diagnosis for their child read information about autism or Asperger's, searching for a fit between their child and the lists of behavior characteristics found in books and on a vast number of websites. None of the lists are a perfect fit, triggering anxiety, confusion, frustration, and even doubt to varying degrees. One website and checklist leads to another and then dozens more. Personal stories, treatment recommendations, and the rules about what should and should not be done quickly pile up in an overwhelming way. Many times the search for the singular family expe-rience through reading information about the autism spectrum on the Internet adds to the family narrative of otherness or isolation. Family stress increases while the parents and other family members process the diagnosis and work towards understanding what it means to enter the autism spectrum culture or world.

Moving Beyond the Global Diagnostic Label with the Singular Presentation Narrative

Families who are finding their way towards integrating a recent autism spectrum diagnosis into their family story benefit greatly from working with clinicians who have the tools to encourage and support the development of their unique and complex story. Their story is not the story of Autism Spectrum Disorder, the global condition. Each family has a story that centers on their singular presentation narrative. Their story is about them, and no other family is living the same story. The narrative therapy process encourages the individuals in the family system to construct individual stories that are multilayered, complex, and transformative. Narrative therapy practices can be useful in guiding individual families through the process of constructing their singular autism spectrum story. This begins when the family is guided away from conceptualizing the diagnosis of the family member as a problem and towards building the story of the unique ways of thinking and being that are part of the individual's autism spectrum brain style. Challenging behaviors that are triggered by sensory sensitivities can then be externalized and discussed in ways that allow curiosity about the form and function of the behavior, leading to the development of practical strategies and supports. This externalization is further supported when the clinician listens closely to the language used by family members when discussing the challenging behaviors. Powerful metaphors can then be created and used to support transformative ways of thinking and responding to stressors.

Identifying the Dominant Story

Each family comes in with a dominant autism spectrum story. For many families, the dominant story centers around limitations on many levels. For parents, the growing realization, for example, that their young child is struggling to develop language and communication skills triggers anxiety and distress. When communication delays are accompanied by the child's self-contained, object-focused style, the sense of dread intensifies. Their natural parenting style and tools leave them with a sense of powerlessness and they struggle as they accumulate experiences with their child that center on limitations; their own limitations and those of their child. These feelings are magnified for parents whose children are highly reactive to sensory stressors, such as daily transition times, sounds, textures, and verbal or social demands. Each time the child encounters a sensory trigger and becomes agitated or distressed, each time the parent unsuccessfully attempts to calm the child, the narrative of limitations anchors into place as the dominant story.

For parents whose children are developing with differences that are not yet clearly identified or defined, the narrative of limitations may extend over many years. Each time a new diagnosis is given, each time a medication is tried and does not have a positive impact on the challenging behaviors, each time the child's school calls for another meeting, the underlying narrative of limitations reverberates through the family system.

The emotions that are experienced by parents who are bound by the limitations narrative often include anxiety, fear, dread, despair, anger, and resentment. As their emotional resources become depleted, a correspondingly negative pattern of communication emerges between family members and may include blaming and isolation. When the narrative of limitations becomes the dominant story it becomes increasingly more difficult for individuals to notice their competencies and successes. The experiences of daily life become emotionally draining instead of energizing and restorative.

Starting the Autism Conversation with Parents

In my practice, when parents call to set up an initial appointment, they are doing more than scheduling a time to come to my office. They are telling their story as we start our "autism conversations." In my initial phone conversation with a parent I start by asking the parent to tell me a bit about his or her child. I write down the key things they say while I listen. After listening for a bit, I thank them for talking about their child and tell them I have been taking detailed notes. Then I tell them what to expect in the first family session: When they come in together I will have some interesting toys or materials available for their child, or, if their child is an older adolescent or young adult, I will start out by talking about a topic of interest to the young person. After taking some time to focus on the interests of the child, adolescent, or young adult, the conversation will expand to a discussion of areas of concern from the point of view of each parent and their child. I tell the parents to expect a two-hour time frame for this conversational arc.

Then I introduce the first narrative document in our therapy conversations: the parent interview.[2] I ask the parents to take their time in answering the questions that I send. I encourage them to include as much detail in their answers as they like, and explain that the details they provide will help me prepare for our sessions. The interview is structured in a way that encourages storytelling. Unlike rating scales and behavior questionnaires, this interview focuses on inviting parents to document the nuanced, unique, and detailed stories that describe their family life.

The process of creating the parent interview document firmly places the singular family story at the center of the conversation. The first meeting becomes an extension of a conversation already started with the family.

Four Key Narrative Shifts

There are four distinctive narrative shifts that are part of the therapy process for families dealing with autism spectrum differences. The narrative therapy process moves the family away from the narrative of limitations in each of the four key areas in a transformative and empowering way.

Although each of the four distinctive narrative shifts form a part of the therapy process for all families, the emphasis varies and depends to some extent on where the family is in the life-cycle process. Families with young children who receive a diagnosis of autism spectrum differences face the transformative challenge of moving from a narrative of *powerlessness to competence*. This narrative shift involves the reconstruction of daily experiences from the perception and sense of powerlessness to that of capability. A key element in this life-changing process is the introduction of language that describes the family experience from the perspective of the child with autism spectrum differences. As parents tell their story, the narrative therapy process provides the clinician with opportunities to help parents notice areas of competency and to introduce empowering language.

As the child moves through childhood and into adolescence, families face the transformative narrative arc of moving from *dysregulated to controlled*. Here the narrative shift involves two main transformations. The first shift occurs when the family is able to reframe the dysregulated behavior patterns as functional for the individual with autism spectrum differences. The second shift follows this externalization and centers on using metaphors to help the individual acquire self-regulation and adaptive responses to stress. The use of visual supports and creating documents are integral parts of this narrative shift.

The executive functioning brain style differences create an additional transformative route for families that can be described as the arc from *prompt-dependency to autonomy*. Working with individuals within the family context is essential to the shift in perceptions necessary to allow for the individual with autism spectrum differences to develop autonomy skills and behaviors while his or her parents redefine their roles.

Finally, the narrative arc of moving from the position of *disorder to style* occurs as the child with autism spectrum differences matures into adulthood. Key elements that promote the shift from disorder to style include shaping the language of self-determination and self-advocacy for the individual with autism spectrum differences as well as for other family members. When the family is seen together, the clinician is able to support the development of multiple, interlocking narratives within the individual and in the family system.

So what does this transformative narrative arc look like when working with families? Let's start with a conversation about the narrative arc families face with young children as they move from an experience of powerlessness to one of capability and competence.

Notes

1   Bruce, Elizabeth J., and Schultz, Cynthia L. (2001). *Nonfinite Loss and Grief: A Psychoeducational Approach*. Baltimore, MD: Brookes Publishing.
2   Monteiro, Marilyn J. (2010). *Autism Conversations: Evaluating Children on the Autism Spectrum Through Authentic Conversations*. Los Angeles, CA: Western Psychological Services; Monteiro, Marilyn J. (2008). *Monteiro Interview Guidelines for Diagnosing Asperger's Syndrome (MIGDAS)*. Los Angeles, CA: Western Psychological Services.

Section II

Guiding Individuals and Families to Develop an Empowered Narrative

3 Powerless to Capable

Shape the Narrative from Powerless to Capable

- Invite the parents to tell their stories through the parent interview document.
- Use sensory toys and materials to start the autism conversation with the child.
- Affirm the parents' expert role in relation to their child.

Respect the Underlying Ambiguous Grief Process

- Support families in processing their mixed emotions about the individual's autism spectrum differences without overtly labeling their process as a form of grief.
- Recognize the power of storytelling in processing underlying ambiguous grief.
- Understand the link between verbalizing anxieties about the individual in the family with autism spectrum differences and the ability to move into feelings of competence.

Model and Shape Perspective-Taking from the Point of View of the Individual with Autism Spectrum Differences

- Powerlessness is diffused when family members are given an accessible way to understand the perspective of the individual with autism spectrum differences.
- Individuals with autism spectrum differences may not be able to represent their perspective and needs to their family members without therapeutic support.
- Use of descriptive language is essential in helping families build a narrative of understanding the individual's autism spectrum differences while helping them move away from labeling and ascribing negative attributes.

From Powerlessness to Competence

"Just so you know, Wyatt probably won't want to come into your office. It's really hard taking him to the doctor." Even over the telephone, the stress level in Naomi's voice came across loud and clear. Naomi was speaking with me to set up a consultation appointment for herself, her husband Patrick, and their four-year-old son. Wyatt's pediatrician encouraged her to come in for a consultation after their last visit to his office.

Wyatt received a diagnosis of autism just prior to his third birthday. When I met him his mother was taking him to weekly sessions with a private speech therapist, an occupational therapist, and a behavior specialist, all of whom specialized in working with children with autism. Naomi and Patrick both held professional positions in their respective fields. Patrick's job required him to travel a great deal, leaving the daily routines and tasks to Naomi. Wyatt was their only child.

"Wyatt is making progress, but we still have a lot of struggles with him at home. He has so much difficulty communicating and gets extremely upset if there is a change in his routine. Being around other people and going places really sets him off. He isn't fully potty trained, and he gets up and roams around at night. We're doing everything possible, but we're exhausted. We want to get him started in a specialized preschool program, but we want to get a better handle on this diagnosis first."

The qualifiers Naomi used in describing daily life at home told the story of how powerless she was feeling.

Over the telephone, Naomi laid out the stressors in a clear and compelling way. As an accomplished professional she was living a life with a marked contrast between her experiences of competency at work and powerlessness at home. She was goal-oriented in both settings, seeking out professionals to provide services to help her son develop critical skills. Her call to me communicated that she and her husband were seeking help in understanding and parenting their son.

"We would like to figure out how to make situations better for him. Well, better for all of us, really."

We discussed what to expect during the consultation visit. I assured Naomi that Wyatt would most likely come into my office with them on the day of their visit and told her that I would plan to greet them with an interesting toy and that I would not speak to Wyatt when they arrived. I explained that the pairing of an interesting toy with limited talking would reduce Wyatt's stress level in the new situation.

I heard Wyatt in the hallway before his parents arrived at my door. He was loudly protesting by vocalizing, using a combination of words and sounds:

"Nooooo! Eeeee, ohhhhh!"

"It's okay Wyatt, you are going to meet the doctor. Sshh, it's okay, Wyatt!" Naomi and Patrick were both repeating their encouragements to their son with frantic overtones.

As they opened the door, I stood at the threshold of the session room with my arm extended while holding a spinning light up toy. It was a plastic globe containing LED lights that lit up when a button on the handle was pushed and the lights spun inside the globe. It made a soft humming sound as it vibrated and as the bright lights emitted changing colorful patterns. I turned it on and off several times, leaving it in the spinning position.

The entryway became quiet, except for Wyatt's parents who continued their nonstop talking.

"Oh, look Wyatt! Look at the lights!"

I held my finger to my lips, signaling for Naomi and Patrick to stop talking. They did. Naomi held Wyatt by the wrist as they faced the spinning light globe. I pressed the button several more times, creating the on and off and then on again pattern. Wyatt approached the globe and when he was close enough to hold it I extended my arm and walked back into my office consultation room. Wyatt entered the room and I handed the globe to him. He took it and held it close to his face while examining the visual details. He pressed it against his cheek and ear as he experienced the vibrations. I held up a second identical globe and walked in front of Wyatt, guiding him and his parents into my office. No one spoke during this time but Wyatt and I were definitely having a conversation. He briefly glanced at me before taking the second globe from me. Even though he "hijacked" the globes so that he was in control of manipulating both of them and eliminated me as a social play partner, he continued to stand in close proximity to me. This was Wyatt's way of communicating that continued interactions that centered on the routine of me providing sensory objects and his exploration of those objects were acceptable. I introduced several toys that created a variety of tactile experiences when squeezed and pressed. Each time I held a toy in the palm of my hand and extended my arm towards Wyatt he reached out and took it. He created a pile of objects on the floor, organizing the objects into distinct categories. Wyatt carefully placed the balls in one pile, the small toys shaped like animals in another pile, and the interlocking blocks in a third pile. Our conversation continued to be a nonverbal, sensory-based exchange. Wyatt's systematic way of thinking and categorizing was clearly emerging.

As part of the preparation process prior to our initial session, I spoke with Naomi on the phone. In our initial conversation I asked questions that invited her to share stories about her son. We discussed the consultation and what she and her husband could expect as they came in as a family. This initial contact was important, as it laid the groundwork for the narrative process. Questions led to stories, and stories provided clues about this family's dominant story about their child and their goals in moving towards a new story.

In addition to the phone conversation, I asked Naomi and Patrick to discuss and complete a detailed parent interview form prior to our first meeting.[1] The interview provided the framework to create a document that reflected a nuanced and multilayered profile of Wyatt. Sending this interview to the parents prior to their first meeting communicated the empowering message that their words, their voices, and their stories were important. The focus centered on the singular family experience, moving away from the global labeling of their child.

Here are some of the observations shared by Wyatt's parents when they completed the parent interview document:

- Most concerned about his language development and ability to talk;
- Concerned about his communication skills (he cannot tell us what he wants using words);
- Overall happy disposition;
- Likes to watch videos and play games on his iPad, especially games with letters and numbers (Starfall, Popmath, Curious George);
- Can play his favorite songs on the keyboard;
- Likes to swing and run around the perimeter of the playground;
- Likes to be around us but does not like having other people in the house (when grandparents and cousins come to visit);
- Hard to manage his distress and sensitivity to certain noises (vacuum cleaner, hair dryer) and crowds;
- Gets upset when people sing or try to have a conversation;
- Gets extremely upset if there is a change in his routine;
- Not fully potty trained;
- Picky eater and selective about clothing;
- Sticks to a routine and gets extremely upset with changes;
- Screams and cries when upset, especially when it is time to stop playing and have a bath or dinner, even after clearly telling him and giving him ample time to prepare;
- Three words to describe him: intelligent, loves music, letters, and numbers, and keeps to himself.

While Wyatt explored the spinning globes and categorized the toys, his parents and I sat down and exchanged greetings. Both Naomi and Patrick were highly verbal and they processed information quickly, moving from one topic to the next and finishing each other's sentences as they intently shared information about their child. Their communication style was in stark contrast to Wyatt's style.

As we began talking, Wyatt began to hum and sing to himself. This became louder the longer we talked. Several times he briefly covered his ears with his fingertips.

"Wyatt is quite a systematic thinker. He is organizing and categorizing the toys by type and has systematically examined the visual details and cause-and-effect properties of each of them." I introduced the descriptive language as I pointed out Wyatt's pattern of behavior as he explored the materials.

"This is how he plays at home. He is constantly putting things together, sometimes in ways that are surprising to us." Highlighting Wyatt's play style invited his parents to describe their son's organizational routine. It gave them a way to talk about their son's competencies instead of his deficits.

"I'm relieved that he is coping so well with coming here today. You knew how to get him in here without stressing him out." Naomi was notably less stressed than she had appeared in the hallway.

"That's because the two of you described Wyatt so well. You told me the types of activities he enjoys." I directed the narrative to highlight Naomi and Patrick's expertise.

"And we noticed that you didn't talk to him when we came in here. We probably talk too much" Patrick added.

"Yes, you and Naomi are highly verbal and express yourselves well. Your natural style is verbal while Wyatt's exploration of the world is three-dimensional. He organizes and explores through visual and tactile exploration of things. In fact, taking in language is stressful for him, making it difficult for you to communicate with him."

"Absolutely. It's frustrating because we know that he understands what we're saying. He's smart. But he refuses to follow our directions." Naomi asserted her input, confirming the established narrative of powerlessness in communicating effectively with her son.

"Let's look at this from Wyatt's perspective for a moment. You described him as having a happy disposition. What I've noticed so far is that when Wyatt manipulates three-dimensional objects he is organizing himself in the world. Things make sense to him as he categorizes things, recognizes letters and numbers, watches preferred videos, and so on. As things make sense to him he feels good and regulates himself, or stays calm. Does that make sense from your point of view?"

"It does, but I hadn't quite thought of it in that way before." Naomi and Patrick listened as they watched Wyatt systematically exploring the materials in front of him.

"Incoming language is a source of stress for Wyatt, even though he understands much of what you are saying. How do we know it's a source of stress? Because every time we begin talking your son begins to hum, or sing, or touch his fingers to his ears. He's done that several times during our conversation today."

"Yes, he does that at home a lot." Patrick confirmed this observation. "It makes it defeating to try and get him to listen and follow directions. The more we talk the harder he resists and then he starts yelling and crying and it's hard to get him to calm down."

"When Wyatt plays, unless he is vocalizing to block out your incoming language, he isn't spontaneously using much language. He truly is organizing his world around the exploration of three-dimensional objects. Language—using it himself and managing your incoming language—is hard work for him. Both you and Wyatt are working hard but your differing styles cancel each other out."

"Huh, that's interesting. Are you saying we set him off? Because that's what it feels like. Doesn't it feel that way to you, Naomi? You're the one who is with him the most."

"It is exactly what it feels like to me but I hadn't put it into words. We do seem to cancel each other out. So how do we fix that?" As Naomi internalized the new framework to understand the communication dilemma she became focused on discovering solutions.

"It's a matter of differing styles. You and Patrick organize in the world through verbal communication. So it's a natural outcome to assume that your son, who understands language, will respond well to verbal communication. For you and Patrick, verbal communication is the most efficient—and natural—way to get things done, while for Wyatt, *seeing* what is coming next is the most efficient—and natural—way to get things done. Language is hard work for him, so he has a lower threshold than you do for managing incoming language."

"So, Naomi, what feels like refusal to you when you give Wyatt directions, may make more sense when we take into account his different communication style. His brain responds to incoming language with agitation and distress because managing incoming language is hard work for him. His brain needs to be shown what is being requested of him while telling him. Showing while telling makes sense to him."

"Now that you mention it, of course it is hard work for him. And we both talk a lot." Naomi glanced at Patrick and he smiled in agreement.

"When you pair your verbal requests with a visual cue, like a picture, you are making your request using Wyatt's natural and strongest communication input: visual. He's much more likely to process what you are asking him to do when you show while telling. Otherwise, you're competing with whatever is capturing his visual attention at the time and it is really hard for him to shift his focus from the visual, organizing event to your words."

"We really want Wyatt to be able to talk and communicate his needs using his words. He is learning more words with his therapist so we want to require him to listen to us and to communicate with us. I worry that if I start using pictures Wyatt won't learn to communicate using his words." Naomi's face communicated how distressing the topic of Wyatt's communication struggles was to her.

Patrick added his thoughts. "So this cancelling each other out; the more we insist that he talk to us the harder he has to work and the more he resists. It's not working for any of us." He turned to Naomi. "This makes sense to me; maybe we should consider making the process easier for Wyatt."

Naomi turned to me. "Are you saying that Wyatt won't stop talking if we start using the pictures and don't talk as much?"

"Think about how your son is using his spontaneous talking now. His verbal communication is most organized when he is labeling things, right?"

"He definitely has a great labeling vocabulary."

"Exactly. Wyatt can organize and retrieve his language best when he has visual context cues. His brain makes sense out of spoken language when the words are paired with visual context cues or visual routines. So using visual supports like pictures and words and pairing your talking with visual directions will actually help Wyatt organize and retrieve his words."

Naomi took in a deep breath and slowly exhaled as her eyes brimmed with tears. "It's just so overwhelming, you know? We're working so hard and I worry so much that we aren't doing enough, or we're not doing the right things."

Patrick reached over and took her hand. "It's been pretty intense. But that's why we're here."

Naomi squeezed Patrick's hand and smiled briefly. "Absolutely." She sighed deeply. "It's just that there are so many opinions out there about what we're supposed to do. We want to make sure that we're not wasting any time in working with Wyatt. At the same time, it seems like he needs some time every day to do what he's doing now." She looked at Wyatt, her gaze taking in her son as he continued his careful inspection of the toys he had grouped into distinct categories.

"With all of the pressures you are feeling, it's hard to remember that no one knows Wyatt better than you do. Today you are learning new ways to talk about Wyatt and how he sees the world but you already know him very well."

"That's true," his mother agreed. "I guess we do know him better than anyone else does."

"Naomi, you told me that Wyatt enjoys matching games, right?"

"He is really good at them. He remembers where things are and what things go together."

"And now he is starting to label letters, numbers, and colors while he plays his matching games, right?"

"He is. Not so much when we ask him to tell us, but more so when he is playing on his own."

"So to help him better anticipate transition times at home and to be less resistant and upset with transitions, using a visual 'first/then' routine paired with your talking would be very helpful for Wyatt."

"And he loves music so maybe we could come up with a song routine to start out with," Naomi added. Expressing her grief about her son's communication differences allowed Naomi to tap into her creative thinking, leading to a restored sense of competency.

We went on to discuss the details regarding a simple plan for Naomi and Patrick to begin using a picture schedule for Wyatt at home. As we did so, Naomi and Patrick actively engaged in the process of revising the narrative they brought into the session with them from powerless to competent. Naomi wrote a list of the main points as we talked.

I also worked with Wyatt, presenting him with additional sensory-based toys and several inset puzzles. Each time I wanted Wyatt to transition to a new activity I showed him the object first and then labeled it. He spontaneously labeled the letters in an alphabet inset puzzle and the colors in the spinning globe. I pointed out Wyatt's organizational style to his parents and modeled the pairing of visual contextual cues with limited language.

As the session came to a close, I asked each of them the same question. "Before we stop, could you tell me one main thing you are taking away from this session?"

Naomi spoke first, referring to her list. "It was really helpful to me when you talked about Wyatt's brain style being visual. You also showed us how well Wyatt responds to visual structure when you had him do the puzzles with you. I don't have the apprehension about using visual supports that I did when I came in here. And I think we'll all be less stressed when we learn how to use tools that make sense to Wyatt."

"Show him while we're telling him. Talk less. Look at things from his perspective," Patrick added.

As Naomi and Patrick left the session the distinct shift in their perspectives was powerfully apparent. The change in their story—the transformation from powerless to capable—was beginning.

Shaping the Narrative Shift from Powerless to Capable

Naomi and Patrick entered the session using language that communicated their sense of powerlessness to effectively communicate with their son. Naomi anticipated that Wyatt would not be able to enter the therapy room or participate in the session in a meaningful way. Their stress level was high. As the session progressed, both of Wyatt's parents were able to apply a new framework to understand communication from their son's perspective. They were also able to describe the complex mix of emotions and pressure for success that held them captive in the powerless narrative. By the end of the session each parent was able to identify key differences in their perspective regarding their approaches to communicating with their son. They were able to see Wyatt's competencies in a new way as well.

What specific narrative tools led to the shift from powerless to capable?

• Part of building a sense of competence is to support the understanding of multiple perspectives and communication styles. This concept was introduced in a powerful way at the start of the session when Wyatt was encouraged to enter the room with a sensory object while minimizing the added stress of incoming language demands.

The narrative of multiple perspectives was supported as Naomi and Patrick's communication style was identified as verbal and contrasted with Wyatt's three-dimensional and visual style. Both styles were identified as competencies.

- Powerlessness is diffused when family members are given an accessible way to understand the perspective of the individual with autism spectrum differences. This narrative shift began to take place when Naomi and Patrick were given the descriptive framework of *"differing styles cancel each other out."* The observation that both Wyatt and his parents were working hard was a key narrative point. Powerlessness is an outcome experienced in a weighty way when people work hard with no results or sense of competence. Wyatt's parents gained an accessible way to understand their son's perspective on communication with the narrative of comparing and contrasting verbal with visual communication as *"the most efficient—and natural—way to get things done."* This shift allowed for what was previously talked about as Wyatt's refusal to follow directions to be understood as *"hard work"* for him.

- Recognizing the link between verbalizing anxieties about the child with autism spectrum differences and the ability to move into feelings of competence is another important narrative tool. For this mother, who was working so hard to help her son develop verbal communication skills, her expressed fear was that using visual communication supports would prevent Wyatt from developing speech. Providing her with a supportive context to express that fear allowed her to articulate her paramount fear and anxiety: *"We're working so hard and I worry so much that we aren't doing enough, or we're not doing the right things."* Expressing this underlying worry helped Naomi feel less isolated and overwhelmed. It provided an opportunity to acknowledge her emotions while introducing the powerful declaration that the parents are experts on their unique and individual child: *"Today you are learning new ways to talk about Wyatt and how he sees the world but you already know him very well."*

- Storytelling is a potent way to help parents process their underlying ambiguous grief about their child's autism spectrum diagnosis. A diagnosis of autism spectrum differences introduces an unclear threat to the family, as the label conjures up generalized anxiety and fear about limitations. How will this diagnosis affect the child's development? What does this mean in terms of the child's participation in everyday events as childhood unfolds into adolescence and adulthood? It takes not only time but also a context to help families adjust to the inclusion of autism into the family story. Storytelling shifts the emphasis from the diagnostic language of autism to the account of the unique individual and his or her family. In Wyatt's case, reminding Naomi that Wyatt enjoys matching games led to her assertion that he is competent in his visual memory skills. She added that he loves music. This led to a discussion of how visual schedules and song routines could be used to support Wyatt's ability to manage transitions in a more successful way. Asking each parent to express *"one main thing you are taking away from this session"* provided an opportunity for Naomi and Patrick to articulate key shifts in their narratives. Parents experience the shift from their powerless to competent narrative when they explicitly describe the essential ideas added to their story through the therapy process.

Note

1 Monteiro, Marilyn J. (2008). *Monteiro Interview Guidelines for Diagnosing Asperger's Syndrome (MIGDAS)*. Los Angeles, CA: Western Psychological Services.

4 Dysregulated to Controlled

Shape the Narrative of Regulation and Control

- Shift the conversational focus away from the language of deficits by inviting parents to describe their child's skills and competencies.
- Frame dysregulated behaviors as reactivity linked to sensory input.
- Provide sensory regulation toys and materials.

Move from Maladaptive to Adaptive Coping Strategies

- Use binary categories to introduce the externalizing concept of using the "reacting" versus the "thinking" part of the brain.
- Link self-regulation tools to metaphors based on the child's area of preferred interest.
- Shape adaptive responses in the individual with autism spectrum differences by alternating tasks within the session.

Fortify the Adaptive Coping Narrative

- Use visual documents when introducing self-regulation tools.
- Introduce the brain training metaphor.
- Build resiliency by helping the family anticipate incremental change and predicting setbacks.

From Dysregulated to Controlled

Many families raising a child with autism spectrum brain differences live under the continual stressor of their child's extreme emotional and behavioral outbursts. The words "meltdown," tantrum," and "blowout" are often used to describe the intense episodic breakdowns that take place at home, in school, and in the community settings. The narrative that quickly surfaces centers around the child's "willfulness." This narrative is most likely to develop when the child is verbally fluent but can occur with less verbal children as well. When the narrative of willfulness becomes entrenched, the child is given powerful labels. Common labels include "out of control," "disrespectful," and "manipulative."

Because the episodes occur in a seemingly unpredictable way, the adults in charge of the child search for ways to explain what is happening. If the child is able to handle transitions sometimes, it becomes confusing when he or she erupts in an intense way at other times. From the perspective of the adult in charge, the situation seems to be the same. Why the meltdown? On some level, isn't the child capable of controlling his or her behavior? Each episode triggers feelings of powerlessness for the adults in charge, intensifying the hardship and forcing the narrative into place of the difficult child with intractable behavior. If the child is able to stop playing a preferred video game sometimes but becomes intensely upset at other times, surely the behavior is manipulative and willful? If the child displays brilliant, logical thinking when discussing his or her areas of interest then surely using logic will work when trying to help the child recognize his or her irrational behavior? When the child with autism only displays extreme behaviors at home and manages to regulate at school, the stress experienced by the parents intensifies, as the unspoken assumption is that the parents are allowing the behavior to occur.

How does the clinician introduce an alternative narrative to this? The dysregulated child with autism spectrum differences oftentimes is labeled as a child with irresolvable behavior problems across settings. Something needs to change. And specifically, the narrative shouts, the child needs to change. Fix him! Fix her!

Nathan and His Parents Make the Narrative Shift from Dysregulated to Controlled

"His school doesn't know what else to do with him and neither do we." The tension in Miles' voice was palpable as he discussed his son.

When I met Nathan he was a ten-year-old boy with a history of explosive behavior episodes. He had received multiple diagnoses, including Attention Deficit Hyperactivity Disorder, Oppositional Defiant Disorder, Anxiety, Depression, and most recently, Pervasive Developmental Disorder, now referred to as Autism Spectrum Disorder. He was under the care of a child psychiatrist and was taking a number of psychotropic medications. Nathan was a capable student. His interests included science, math, and computer games that required perceptual reasoning skills. He was well versed in the language of Minecraft and Terraria but notably less so in the social language required for fluid, back-and-forth conversations with others. Nathan was often dismissive of others, and did not seem to recognize the difference between children and adults. He had little patience when it came to the behavior of his classmates and frequently became irritated and agitated when he perceived a peer to be deviating from the rules or possibly teasing him. He frequently argued with his teachers, pointing out minor inconsistencies in their directions or explanations regarding course content.

Recently at his school Nathan became enraged when one of his teachers emphatically told him to stop arguing and return to his seat. As his behavior escalated the teacher directed Nathan to leave the classroom and go to the office, which he refused to do. His agitated behaviors included shouting, screaming, standing in the personal space of the teacher, pulling on her sleeve, shaking his fist, crying, stomping his feet, pacing the room, and kicking chairs and other classroom objects. He had to be escorted physically from the room and continued to rage for over an hour before he calmed down. Once he was calm he stated that he wanted to go back to his class but did not want to talk about what had happened.

Nathan's parents told similar stories about their son's behavior at home. They identified several triggers for Nathan's behavioral outbursts. When he was playing one of his beloved games and it was time to do something else the transition from the preferred activity frequently led to agitated behavior. When Nathan perceived an error or a discrepancy in a comment made by an adult or a peer, his perception would often lead to argumentative and then increasingly dysregulated behavior. Once upset, Nathan's enraged behavior could last for an hour or longer before he was able to calm down. Sometimes he began to calm down, but then his agitation flared up again before the episode was finished. Each time an episode completed its arc, Nathan resumed his energetic and pleasant disposition. When the adults tried to revisit the incident that triggered the episode Nathan responded to queries by stating: "I have no idea."

Nathan, his father Miles, and his mother Paige came in together. Nathan had dark, slightly disheveled hair and a sturdy build. He was wearing sweatpants and a long sleeved shirt depicting the periodic table of elements using Minecraft images under each symbol. The heading on the shirt read "Periodic Table of Minecraft." His eyes took in the room and when he noticed the magnet pieces and corresponding puzzle books he enthusiastically loped towards them and began manipulating the pieces.

"Excellent! Actual magnets."

"The yellow pieces fit together to make a 'y ball.' It's quite difficult to figure out but I think you are up for the challenge."

"If you mean this puzzle is no match for my excellent brain then you are correct!"

Paige nodded her head, a grim expression on her face. "Nathan, you can probably figure that out but if it's too hard don't get upset."

"I'm not going to get upset! Just let me concentrate!" Nathan turned his back to his parents and placed his head close to the pieces as he methodically and systematically put them together into their various configurations.

This activated his father. "Don't talk to your mother like that, Nathan. Show some respect!"

Miles turned to me. "You see what we have to deal with here. As long as everything goes his way Nathan is happy. But the world doesn't work that way."

"So would you say that being flexible, that is to say, shifting from his agenda to the agenda of others, is difficult for him?"

"If you mean does he want to do what he wants to do all of the time, then yes."

"And when he is doing what he wants to do, he does what?"

"Plays games, reads books, watches videos . . . oh, and monopolizes the conversation, telling us about his games or science facts. Right now it's all about matter and anti-matter." Miles frowned as he listed his son's preferences.

Nathan, who was clearly listening, joined the conversation without turning around. "Anti-atoms, not anti-matter. Anti-matter is made of anti-atoms." He held his arms out, palms raised. He lifted his right palm. "Matter." He lifted his left palm. "Anti-matter." Then slapped his hands together. "Annihilation! Energy is released!" He went back to building with the magnets.

Both of his parents watched their son as he played out a routine they had clearly seen before.

Miles looked at me. "He says that a lot lately."

He directed his next comment to Nathan.

"That's what we're talking about, Buddy. Living with you is like waiting for the matter to collide." Miles used a familiar tone in addressing his son.

"You mean living with me is like waiting for the matter and the *anti*-matter to collide. Like the Hadron Collider."

Paige rolled her eyes. "Arrgghh! Enough details already! It's impossible for this family to stay on point."

"And what is the point, Paige, that your son and husband seem to be missing?" I asked.

"That something needs to change. I can't keep doing this! It's a monumental effort to get Nathan through the day and there is always something that sets him off."

"Tell me more."

"Nathan needs my help to get up in the morning, to get his things ready, to get to school. I have to give him so many reminders that I'm worn out. And when Miles is around it really aggravates him when Nathan doesn't cooperate. Then the two of them get into it."

"On the rare occasions when you're not working much harder than your son to get him organized and out the door, tell me some of the times you enjoy together."

Paige's eyes welled with tears. "I love Nathan. He's incredibly aggravating but he's a great kid. I am constantly amazed by his comments about the nature of the universe. And he can be very affectionate. He doesn't like it when I get mad or upset."

"Tell me about what you enjoy doing with your mom, Nathan."

Nathan had been sitting quite still while his mother talked. He turned halfway around before speaking. "Well, naturally I like talking to her. And I like to show her new things like the biomes I've been adding to my Terraria. I just built an awesome sky bridge."

"So you like it when she shares your world with you; your interests?"

"Well, technically, I like it when she shares the worlds I'm creating with my games. And I like it when we read together."

"How about with your Dad, Nathan? What do the two of you enjoy together?"

"Well with my dad I like to build things. And look stuff up on the Internet."

I turned to Miles. "What are you and Nathan building now?"

"We're building a planetary model of the atom using wire and Styrofoam balls."

"Technically we're building the *Bohr* model, Dad."

"He wants to hang it from his ceiling."

Paige jumped in. "See what I mean? Those two either fight or they get caught up in science projects."

"So when you share Nathan's interests with him there is some time that each of you enjoy one another's company."

"Yes, we do. It's living with him that is so hard."

"Nathan, I'd like to tell you something I've noticed about you and you can tell me if you agree. Okay?"

"That would be acceptable."

"Well, for one thing, you are a boy who is quite a scientific thinker. Your brain style is a scientific one."

"That is correct. I will be an astrophysicist when I grow up."

"Excellent! That goal makes logical sense, given your interests now."

Nathan stood still, gazing off to the side. He waited for me to continue.

"So with your scientific brain style, I'm guessing that you like it when things are logical and predictable. When things follow predictable rules and patterns."

"That is also correct." He paused. "I wish the whole world followed the rules of physics instead of dealing with these random variables ALL THE TIME!" He shook his fists and grimaced as he loudly finished his statement.

I turned to his parents. "When I say that Nathan is a scientific thinker, I mean that his brain style is most comfortable with facts and information." I turned back to Nathan. "And part of the scientific brain style means that you are also a binary thinker. Things are either one thing or the opposite, with nothing in between."

"That's correct. Zeros and ones. Matter and anti-matter."

"Does that describe Nathan?" I asked his parents.

"Absolutely. He is a totally 'black or white' thinker. Nothing in between," Paige agreed.

Miles raised his eyebrows and grinned. "Binary thinker, huh? Kind of like me." He turned to Nathan. "Kind of like both of us, right, Buddy?"

"Correct again. Maybe that's why we're so combustible sometimes."

His dad snorted. "Speak for yourself. You're the combustible one in this family."

"Remember when I mentioned earlier that it might be difficult for Nathan to be flexible? To shift from his agenda to yours? Binary thinkers have to learn—to train their brains—to be flexible."

I drew a T on the notepad on the table. "Nathan, here's a binary chart. Let's show one thing that typically happens to binary thinkers before they train their brains to be flexible." Nathan fixed his gaze on the page and I continued. "When you are calm—when the world makes sense and you are doing the things you enjoy—you are using the *thinking* part of your brain. Your brain is in *thinking* mode." I wrote the word "thinking" on the left side of the T-chart.

"But then when something unexpected happens—when you are deeply focused on your game and you have to stop; when your teacher makes an incorrect statement—you switch from the thinking part of your brain to the *reacting* part of your brain." I wrote the word "reacting" on the right side of the T-chart.

"Does this make sense to you, Nathan?"

"You are correct. I have two sides."

"Thinking," I touched the word on the chart.

"And reacting," Nathan touched the word on the chart.

I turned to his parents. "Does this make sense to you?"

"Definitely."

"So, Nathan, when you are in the thinking part of your brain, your words and actions make logical sense. You can follow directions, ask for clarification, and so on. And most of the time, when you are in the thinking part of your brain, can you identify the way you feel inside?"

Nathan furrowed his brow and placed his index finger on his chin. "Well, let me see . . . calm . . . and happy."

I wrote the words "calm" and "happy" in the "Thinking" column. I also wrote "follow directions" and "ask for clarification."

"But when you switch to the reacting part of your brain. . ."

Before I could continue, Nathan slapped his hands together and exclaimed, "Annihilation!"

"Exactly. When the reacting part of your brain takes over, everything changes. What happens to your ability to stay calm and logical?"

He repeated his "annihilation" routine.

"So your ability to use your words goes away, right?"

Nathan nodded. I wrote down "loses words" in the "Reacting" column.

"And the way you feel inside? Can you identify how that changes?"

"Super Nova!" He paused a moment to think. "Super mad. Super frustrated."

I wrote those three descriptors on the chart.

"And your actions change, too, don't they?"

Nathan processed that for a moment before speaking. "I have no idea."

When Nathan used this phrase in a rote way, it was his way of signaling that his threshold for managing this conversation was being breached.

"Talking about this is hard work, Nathan. I admire you for working on this today. Shall we put this on pause for a few minutes, talk about something else, and then come back to it?"

"Excellent! Hey, let me show you how to put the 'y ball' together. The key is to match the pieces with the dots to the pieces without the dots." Nathan thrust the finished magnet ball close to my face as he explained the pattern.

"Awesome! Let me show you this other ball that has some interesting properties." I picked up a plastic ball called a "Switch Pitch" that flipped from one color to another when thrown. I handed the ball to Nathan and urged him to throw it to his father. Nathan threw the ball a bit awkwardly and with a great deal of force, but his father caught it. Miles threw it back to Nathan, and the ball switched colors. Instead of continuing the game with his father, when Nathan caught the ball he turned away as he closely examined it.

"Let me see . . . how does this work . . . oh! The velocity forces the air through these interfaces, causing the shift from the blue side to the red side. Excellent!"

I picked up the pad with the T-chart again. "So, Nathan. There are two things I need your help with before we stop today. May I tell you what they are?"

"Yes."

"The first one is to talk about one more part of this brain chart. I'll show you the second one when we finish this."

Nathan stood beside me and I continued. "Tell me three actions you do when the reacting part of your brain takes over. I wrote the numbers 1, 2, and 3 on the T-chart in the "Reacting" column.

Nathan once again furrowed his brow and raised his index finger to his chin. "Well, let me see . . . sometimes I yell . . . sometimes I kick things . . . and sometimes I SHAKE MY FIST LIKE THIS!!!" He raised his voice while he shook his fist and grimaced, clear signs that he was finished with this dysregulating task.

I had written down each action as he described it. "Well done, Nathan! We're finished with this brain chart." I ripped the page off the pad and held it in front of him. "Who would you like to hold on to this to take it home?"

Nathan took the paper and walked over to his mother. "You are in charge of this."

"Okay Nathan. Thanks."

"Nathan, I told you we have one other thing for us to do today. I will need your scientific brain to help me though."

Nathan approached me, ready to assist. "Let's make a scale that shows how your brain works, starting with when you are calm and thinking and going to where you are "super nova" and reacting. I drew a line on the page and wrote the number 1 on the far left and the number 5 on the far right.

"Here's where I need your brain. Do you want this scale to represent atoms, or the universe expanding, or . . ."

"Atoms splitting and atoms colliding!" Nathan interrupted.

"Excellent!" I wrote: "atoms splitting" under the number 1 and "atoms colliding" under the number 5. "What about number 2?"

Nathan did not have to think for very long. "Oh, that should be 'atoms forming elements.' It's the natural order of things!" Clearly he had thought about atoms quite a bit, as his sentences had a scripted quality to them. He was fully engaged now, and as I moved my pencil to the number 3 he spontaneously offered the descriptor.

"And next the atoms form into matter . . . and then they collide!" He frowned as he examined the chart. "Hey, wait! That's only four steps. We have to add the last step!"

I wrote: "atoms form matter" under number 3. He directed me to move "atoms colliding" from under number 5 to under number 4.

"And now, we're ready for NUMBER FIVE!" Nathan raised his fists and took a deep breath. "NUCLEAR FISSION!!!" He punched his fists into the air and jumped up and down.

This level of intensity activated his parents. "Nathan, quiet down! You're too loud!" Paige used a hissing voice as she pleaded with Nathan to calm down. He did not appear to respond to her.

I took a deep breath in an exaggerated way, capturing Nathan's attention. When I spoke I spoke in a quiet voice. "You did it, Nathan. You named each point on your scale. Well done." I silently held the scale up for him to examine, giving him time to regroup without further demands.

"Now, Nathan, can you point to where on this scale your words and actions are at this exact moment?" He held the paper and frowned for a moment. "I would say that at this exact moment I am a level 2."

"Atoms forming . . . and what feeling can we link to that number?"

"You could say that level is calm, happy. Not super calm or super happy, but calm and happy."

"So let's write those under level 2."

"You mean 'number 2.'"

"Good point, Nathan. Actually, each number represents a level, correct?"

"You could say that."

"So let's think about each of these five levels as levels you can identify for how you are thinking and feeling. If level 2 is calm and happy, what feelings go under level 1?"

"I already told you that. Super calm and super happy."

"That's correct, you did tell me that. Let's write those down." I did. "And you also already talked about your feelings at level 5. You said . . . "

"Annihilation! Energy release!"

"Yes, and also 'super mad' and . . ."

"Super frustrated." Nathan finished my sentence for me and I wrote the descriptors on the scale.

"That leaves levels 3 and 4. What should we put under level 4?"

Nathan looked at the scale for a moment. "Uh, mad? Frustrated?"

"That sounds like a good plan. Maybe we could also add the word 'agitated?'"

"Okay. Add that."

"And last level to add a word is level 3. How about the word 'neutral?'"

"And also 'so-so.'"

Our finished scale looked like this:

1	2	3	4	5
Atoms split	Atoms form elements	Atoms form matter	Atoms collide Heavy nucleus splits	Nuclear fission Annihilate! Energy release!
Super calm Super happy	Calm Happy	Neutral So-so	Mad Frustrated Agitated	Super mad Super frustrated

"And, now, Nathan, you can use this scale to help you control your level. You will have to train your brain. The first step in training your brain is learning to recognize your level." I handed him the scale we had created together. This time, instead of taking it to his mother, Nathan held on to the paper.

I turned to his parents. "This is hard work for Nathan. He did a great job."

Miles quickly agreed. "Nathan, buddy, I am really proud of you. We'll help you train your brain."

Paige agreed. "Train his brain . . . I like that. We can help him do that." She turned to her son. "What do you think, Nathan? Maybe instead of telling you to calm down I can ask you to tell me your level?"

"That is a good plan."

It was time to help the family anticipate incremental change and to predict setbacks. I had already introduced the concept of "hard work" along with the concept of "brain training."

"So tell me one thing you got out of our conversation today, Paige."

Paige looked thoughtful before she spoke. "There are so many things . . . but the main thing is now we have someplace to start. These . . ." She waved the T-chart a few times in the direction of the scale Nathan was holding for emphasis. ". . . are concrete ways to help Nathan learn what he needs to say and do. I realized today, watching him talk with you, that it really is hard for him to use his words to express himself when he gets upset."

"It is hard work for Nathan. Using the T-chart and rating scale to help Nathan identify and practice using the replacement 'words and actions' will definitely help him reduce the intensity and physical nature of his 'reacting' times. It will take work and practice, though."

Paige nodded. "His blow ups have been happening all of his life. It's not going to change overnight; we know that. But now I can see that it's possible that Nathan might be able to learn how to control his reactions better. What do you think, Nathan?"

Nathan held up the paper with his scale and nodded his head several times in a rhythmical way. "This could work."

I turned to Miles. "What did you get out of this meeting, Miles?"

Miles sighed deeply. "I'm not going to lie to you. I came in here thinking this would probably be a rehash of what we already knew. But this helped me understand how Nathan's brain works. I could see it when I watched him talking with you. For someone who is as smart as he is and knows as much as he does it really is hard work for him to explain what happens to him when he goes ballistic." He paused. "If we can help him learn to control his reactivity it will change his life . . . and ours."

Miles struggled to maintain his composure before continuing. "My biggest fear is that if Nathan doesn't learn to get control over himself, he will end up in jail or in some sort of, I don't know, institution."

He swallowed and sighed, looking at his son. "All we want is for you to be able to get a handle on this, Nathan. We'll do whatever it takes to help you."

Nathan walked over to his father and stood beside him. They put their arms around each other and Nathan put his head on his father's shoulder.

"Nathan, your dad and mom get you, don't they?" I asked.

Nathan nodded. "Our molecules fit together." He lifted his head up and tensed his body in an exaggerated way. "Except when they don't! Then . . ." He slapped his hands together: "Annihilation!"

"But now, Nathan, you are going to train your brain to stop the process before you get to 'annihilation!' May I see your scale again?"

He brought the scale over to me and we looked at it together. "For this next week, Nathan, practice using your scale to train your brain to check on where you are during the day: in the morning, during the school day, when you get home, and before bed. Will you agree to do that?

Nathan nodded once, emphatically.

"Your parents will help by asking you what number fits how you are feeling at various times during the day. Right, parents?"

Paige and Miles agreed.

"So for this week, Nathan, see if you can stop the cycle before you get to a full blown 5. Let's list two things you can do to keep things below level 5. First let's list one thing you can *say*. Then we'll list one thing you can *do*."

"Well, I could say to my atoms: 'Calm down; no need to collide' or something like that."

"Excellent! Talk to the atoms." I wrote that on his scale under level 3. "Now what is one thing you can *do*?"

"Well, let's see. I could . . ." he frowned and then his face brightened. "I could take my atoms for a walk! That way they will be in motion without the risk of imminent collision!"

"Great idea! Walk back and forth, and concentrate on calming down those atoms." I wrote: "take my atoms for a walk" on his scale. "You know, when you take your atoms for a walk you are releasing energy before they have to collide or reach annihilation. That is a great idea, Nathan."

"I want to ask you about two more ways to keep your atoms from colliding. Okay?"

"Okay."

"You could also calm your atoms down by clenching your fists really hard and holding them for the count of five before releasing them. Show me how that would work."

Nathan clenched his fists and his face contorted into a forceful grimace while he counted to five and then splayed his fingers in a rigid posture.

"You could also take five deep breaths, expelling the air with force at the end of each breath. Show me how that would work."

With exaggerated facial and body tensing Nathan demonstrated the action.

"Excellent! You now have three actions you can use to keep your atoms from colliding." I wrote these actions on his scale.

I turned to his parents. "At home, when Nathan is getting up to a level 3 or 4, remember to stop talking to him and give him some time to regroup without having to process your incoming language demands."

I turned to Nathan. "Nathan, let's come up with something your parents can say to help you get yourself back to level 3 or lower. Maybe something like: 'Tell me your level right now' or: 'Tell me when you're back at level 3?'"

Nathan thought about that. "They should ask me my level. And they should also tell me to 'take a walk and have your talk,' meaning my talk with my atoms, of course."

"Let's see how that works. Remember that it will take practice, and that it will be work for all of you. Also, remember that your brain has been reacting for a long time. That's what it is used to doing. You will have to practice to train it to follow your new plan."

They all agreed. I turned to Nathan one last time.

"So, Nathan. What is one thing you learned in here today?"

"That I can possibly keep my atoms from colliding and annihilating everything." After a pause he held up the yellow magnet ball. "And I have excellent magnet building skills!"

Shaping the Narrative Shift from Dysregulated to Controlled

Now let's discuss the therapy conversation with Nathan and his parents from the narrative point of view. When the session began, Page and Miles described a household where the predominant themes were powerlessness and dysregulation. Nathan was disengaged from the discussion. As the session progressed, Nathan took increasing responsibility for the development of a self-regulation plan while his parents found a positive framework to understand their son's dysregulated behavior. This framework also helped them shift from a sense of being powerless to sense of feeling capable.

What specific narrative tools led to this family shift?

- The concept of flexibility was introduced (*"shifting from his agenda to the agenda of others"*). This replaced the negative frame of "doing what he wants to do all of the time."

- The emphasis was placed on encouraging the parents to describe Nathan's interests instead of talking about his deficits. This provided a building block to introduce the brain style story line (*"scientific thinker"*; *"binary thinker"*).

- Demands for Nathan's participation in the verbal discussion were minimized at the start of the session. Instead, he was encouraged to explore the magnets. This allowed him to listen to and process the concepts being introduced before his participation was required.

- When the conversation organized around his parents discussing what they enjoyed doing with him, Nathan was invited to tell what he enjoyed doing with each of his parents. This placed the emphasis on Nathan's shared interests and competencies.

- The conversation with Nathan was structured to create maximum predictability. This was accomplished by two repeating conversational structures. The first was telling him the structure of the upcoming conversation or request (*"I'd like to tell you something*

I've noticed and you tell me if you agree." "There are two things I need your help with before we stop today."). The second was systematically asking him to confirm his agreement with each concept as it was introduced (*"Does this make sense to you, Nathan?" "So your ability to use your words goes away, right?"*).

- Visual documents were used to structure the conversation about self-regulation (the T-chart and the self-regulation scale). Nathan's interest in atoms was used to anchor the regulation scale in one of his areas of preferred interest.

- Nathan was given a choice regarding who the keeper of the documents should be. He chose his mother for the T-chart but kept the self-regulation scale. This conversational pattern kept him engaged, as it provided him with repeated binary decision points and a sense of conversational predictability and control.

- Conversational demands centering on the discussion of self-regulation were alternated with redirection to the manipulative materials (the magnets and the "switch pitch"). This allowed Nathan to regroup when he began to experience dysregulation (when he spoke in a louder voice and used exaggerated expressions). Monitoring his threshold for incoming language demands, redirection to the preferred materials and topics, and mirroring Nathan's speaking style led to his sustained attention and ability to participate in the completion of the two regulation tools during the family session.

- Descriptive language was modeled throughout the session. When Nathan became dysregulated and repeated his *"Annihilation!"* routine, this was identified with the descriptive question: *"So your ability to use your words goes away, right?"* The terms *"brain style," "thinking part of your brain," "reacting part of your brain,"* and *"train your brain"* helped Nathan and his parents externalize his pattern of explosive behavior, giving each of them a sense of control and optimism about helping Nathan make the shift from dysregulated to controlled.

5 Prompt-Dependence to Autonomy

Shape an Understanding of Executive Functioning Development

- Introduce the narrative of executive functioning and autonomy skills as "hard work" for the autism brain style.
- Identify the thinking skills that need to be systematically taught and practiced to promote autonomy.
- Highlight the role sensory differences play in the child's prompt-dependency.

Parents and Their Role as the Externalized Executive Functioning Brain

- Help parents understand the role they play as the externalized executive functioning brain for the child with autism spectrum differences.
- Operationalize the goal of shifting the work load from the parent to the child.
- Model the use of visual supports that promote flexibility during the therapy session.

Shifting from Prompt-Dependence to Autonomy and Self-Advocacy

- Introduce the narrative of brain training.
- Use documents to support the development of independence in completing daily routines.
- Build resiliency by predicting the fluctuations and inconstancy that are an inherent part of the skills acquisition process.

From Prompt-Dependence to Autonomy

Parents play a key role in their child's progression from prompt-dependence to autonomy. Neuro-typical children acquire executive functioning skills over the course of childhood and adolescence, allowing them to gain autonomy while completing age-appropriate developmental tasks.[1] Children developing with autism spectrum brain style differences struggle to manage daily routines. Getting out of bed, brushing teeth, dressing, bringing home school assignments—many of these daily routines become monumental challenges that place the parent in the role of organizer, planner, and enforcer. It seems to parents that they are working much harder than their child to move the child through the details of daily life. It becomes difficult to imagine that the child will ever be able to complete simple actions without close supervision and constant support. The undercurrent of anxiety for parents is powerful, as they worry about whether their child will be able to function independently as an adult. This narrative plays a major role in the arc of family life.

At the same time, it is frustrating and confusing for parents of children with autism spectrum differences when their child displays the clear ability to initiate, plan, and problem-solve in his or her areas of preferred interest. Complex levels of games become mastered, facts about marine life or dinosaurs are committed to memory, and release dates of movies are planned months in advance. This uneven pattern of development makes the daily process of organizing, planning, and enforcing self-care routines all the more puzzling and frustrating.

So what exactly are the executive functioning skills children need to move successfully from prompt-dependence to autonomy? Children need to acquire the ability to *inhibit* impulses to sustain their focus and attention on nonpreferred tasks. Problem solving depends on the child's ability to *inhibit* impulses, along with his or her ability to use *working memory*; that is to say, to hold multiple pieces of information in memory at the same time so they can be used to complete a task. The executive functioning skills of *flexible thinking, planning*, and *organization* are also required. Finally, completing tasks and routines depends on the child's ability to *initiate* goal-directed behavior and to *regulate* his or her emotional responses.[2] Simple daily tasks, such as dressing, homework, and getting ready to leave the house on time require executive functioning skills.[3]

In families with typically developing children, parents provide a progressive degree of prompting and support. Young children require hands-on support while older children and adolescents require verbal prompts and reminders, along with some incentives and consequences. As the child's brain develops, increasingly complex tasks can be mastered and managed with decreasing degrees of prompt-dependence.

In families with a child on the autism spectrum the need for close supervision and prompting becomes protracted and a sense of progression is lost. The autism brain simply does not provide the developmental sequence of inhibition, working memory, flexibility, planning, organization, initiation, and regulation that allows for a progressive increase in autonomy.[4] Before the shift from prompt-dependence to autonomy can be made successfully, these skills must be systematically taught and practiced.

Understanding the child's sensory differences is an additional factor that enters into helping a child with autism spectrum differences develop his or her executive functioning skills. To what degree does the child experience sensory sensitivities to touch, texture, movement, visual input, or sound? To what degree do his or her areas of preferred interest capture the child? And finally, how much inflexibility does the child experience when he or she is required to shift from one activity to the next?

Sara and Her Mother Make the Narrative Shift from Prompt-Dependence to Autonomy

Sara, a tall, slender 11-year-old girl with long, wavy, walnut brown hair contrasted sharply with her mother Deana. Sara glided into the room with her eyes slightly downcast, gazing to the side. Her face and demeanor reflected her detachment from her surroundings and emphasized her attention to her interior world. Her mother was clearly grounded in the here and now, with a steady gaze, and a serious, focused presence.

Sara sat briefly in a chair but as the conversation began she drifted to the floor, where she sat with her favorite animal figurines from The Littlest Pet Shop. It was difficult for Sara to share conversational details about her preferred topic but she held up each of her figurines and stated a fact about each one when I prompted her to share her figurines with me. Unless I prompted interactions or responses Sara showed a preference for solitary play. Her interest in the figurines was like that of a much younger child, as she sat on the floor and acted out scenes while softly humming and talking in a self-directed way. Sara had some strong academic skills in the areas of reading and math calculations so her play skills were a reflection of her autism spectrum brain style differences and not due to global developmental delays. In addition to her figurines, Sara enjoyed drawing pictures of characters from The Littlest Pet Shop and watching videos about the characters. She was also interested in animals and enjoyed reading books and watching videos about mammals and marine life. She had received a diagnosis of autism when she was five years old.

"It's just the two of us at home and that's a good thing because we would never manage to get out of the house if I had somebody else to get ready besides her. Honestly, I thought by now she would be able to get herself ready in the morning." Deana glanced over to Sara as she finished her sentence.

I looked at Sara as well, or at her back because she was now positioned in such a way that she was turned away from us. "Tell me more. Is it the getting started on her own that is hard, or is it also keeping it going and finishing what she's started?"

"Both. She needs to have me right there to get out of bed, put her clothes on, brush her teeth. She won't start until I'm in her room and if I leave she just stops until I come back. It's incredibly frustrating. If I leave her alone she gets caught up in her play and forgets what she's supposed to be doing." Deana frowned while reflecting on this. "People have told me to take away all of her Pet Shop things and I tried that. It didn't make any difference. Sara is just as happy to lie there and think about her stuff and it doesn't make it any easier to get her started."

"So getting started is really hard for Sara. She depends on you to help her get started every day."

"Getting started and following through."

"You are having to work harder than Sara at getting started and following through."

Deana nodded in agreement. "Absolutely. Much harder."

"What are your thoughts about what might be getting in the way of Sara's being able to get started and to follow through?"

"Honestly, I think her anxiety gets in the way. She'd prefer not leaving the house and she'd like to stay home with her things all of the time."

Although her back was turned, Sara was clearly listening to our conversation. Her humming had stopped, and she held her figurines but was no longer having them act out a scene.

"Sara, may I ask you a question?" I waited until she responded before continuing. Sara nodded and moved her head so that I could see her profile.

"Tell me the one you like more: staying home or going to school."

Sara responded immediately and swung around to face her mother. "Staying home! Mom, can you home school me? Please, please, please?" Sara got on her knees and put her hands in front of her like paws. She waved them up and down while vigorously nodding her head.

Deana did not respond but raised an eyebrow while looking at me.

"Sara, I'm guessing you have asked your mom that question before, right?"

Sara continued to nod vigorously but turned towards me. "And I'm guessing she told you she has to work and you have to go to school, right?"

Sara gave an exaggerated sigh and dropped her hands to her sides. She frowned. "But I don't like going to school. I want to stay home."

"Tell me two things that you do not like about school, Sara." I held up a finger to signal the first thing.

Sara thought for a few seconds. "Too much work."

I raised a second finger.

"Too many people."

"So, school is hard work. Hard work for you to do all of the assignments. Hard work to be around so many people." I paused. "And hard work to be away from your favorite things, like Littlest Pet Shop."

"Yes!" Sara agreed.

"And getting you ready for school in the morning is hard work for your mom, right Sara?"

"But she's my mommy!" Sara slid over beside her mother and rested her head on her mother's knee. Deana reached out and gently smoothed Sara's hair.

"Of course! She's a great mommy too, isn't she?" Sara slowly nodded her head up and down while continuing to rest it on her mother's knee.

"But, Sara, I just thought of something!" I said.

She raised her head. "What?"

"Well, you are 11 years old, right?"

"Yes, so. . ." she raised her shoulders.

"So maybe your mom needs your help figuring out how you can get started in the mornings a little more on your own." I paused. "Let's ask her."

Sara looked at her mother. "Do you?"

"Do I what, Sara?"

"Do you want me to help you figure out how to get me started?"

"That would be great."

"Because, Sara, I'm guessing that some of your favorite characters in the Littlest Pet Shop take care of pets and teach them to take care of themselves, right?"

Sara nodded once again.

I picked up a notepad and a pencil. "Let's make a list that shows us how much help you are needing from your mom right now. . ." I wrote the words "Mom help now" on the upper left side of the paper and drew a line down the middle of the page.

"And then let's make a list of how you and your mom will figure out how you can help yourself." I wrote the words "Help myself" on the upper right side of the paper.

"Let's start with getting out of bed in the morning. Tell me what your mom has to do now to get you out of bed."

"Well, she sits on my bed and rubs my legs and tells me it's time to get up."

I turned to Deana. "Is that what you do?"

Deana nodded. "That's what I do. Every morning."

"And does that do it? Do you get up on your own after that, Sara?" I asked.

Deana snorted.

Sara answered. "No, she has to pull off all of my covers and sometimes pull my legs to get me out of bed."

"And when that happens are you calm and cooperative?"

"When that happens I kick and yell. But I finally get out of bed." She demonstrated by kicking her legs wildly in the air.

"And do you like to kick and yell before you get out of bed, Sara?"

"Not really. I don't like to get upset."

"That's true," Deana added. "You fight me getting out of bed but I know it's no fun for you either. It's just not a good way to start the day for either of us."

"So let me ask you this: It sounds like the part where your mom sits on your bed and rubs your legs feels good. Is that right, Sara?"

Sara nodded.

I turned to Deana. "Is that part okay with you?"

"Yes, I don't mind waking Sara up and rubbing her legs. I just want her to get out of bed and get going without a fight."

"So Sara, it sounds to me like we need to come up with a plan that will help you train your brain to get started in the morning. Kind of like your Pet Shop characters train their pets. They do that, right?"

"Oh yes, they have to take care of their pets and teach them things."

"So your brain doesn't know how to get started on its own yet. Your brain waits for your mom to get you started. But now that you are 11 years old it's time for you to train your brain to get started on its own." I paused. "Do you think that is something you can do? Train your brain?"

Sara nodded. She glanced towards her mother who nodded as well.

"So I noticed, Sara, that you like to use your figures to act out scenes that you remember from your shows. That looks like a lot of fun." I paused. "And your brain is really good at remembering the details and playing out the scenes, right?"

Sara nodded.

"And when you act out scenes that you remember from your shows, does that feel good or bad?"

"Good."

"So getting out of bed in the morning is kind of the same thing. You will be acting out a scene, remembering the details, and playing them out as you get out of bed."

"Maybe you could decide which character you are going to be most like when you get out of bed and get ready for school. Then you could pretend to be like that character while you get ready." I paused and continued. "What do you think about that idea?"

"Like Blythe Baxter?"

Deana served as the interpreter for this comment. "Blythe is Sara's favorite character because Blythe has a special bond with animals. She also goes to school, right, Sara?"

Sara nodded. "She lives in the big city with her dad. She's a teenager."

"Wonderful! So Sara, you could train your brain to get out of bed and get started in the morning by acting out the scene the way Blythe would act. Like a teenager. Could you imagine doing that brain training, Sara?"

"Uh huh. That would be fun."

"More fun than being pulled out of bed kicking and screaming," Deana added.

I returned to the notepad. "So Sara, let's put 'kicking and screaming' in this column and 'Littlest Pet Shop brain training' in this one."

Sara watched intently as I wrote in each column.

She stood close to the paper. "You can just write 'LPS.' That's what we call it."

"Thank you, Sara. I'm glad to know that fact."

"Sara, I noticed that you pay attention to how things look. For instance, you notice all the special details with your figurines. And you draw them in detail, too, right?"

Sara nodded.

"So it might really help if you drew a story about you getting up in the morning and training your brain to act out the scene. Maybe you and your mom could work on that. What do you think?"

"I could do that with mom."

"So maybe you could pick the four main things you need to do by yourself in the morning and include those in your drawing and story."

I wrote the numbers one through four in the right-hand column. I wrote: "get out of bed" beside number one.

"Sara, what is the second thing you need to do on your own once you get out of bed?" I asked.

"Go to the bathroom."

"And do you do that by yourself now?"

"Of course."

Deana added, "But you usually get back into bed after that, and we start all over again with the kicking and screaming. Unless I stand there and block the bed when you come out of the bathroom."

I wrote "bathroom" on the list.

"Sara, after you come out of the bathroom, what's the third thing you have to do to get ready for school?"

"Get dressed. Then eat breakfast. Then get my backpack. Then go to school."

"Excellent! Let's put all of those on the list." I added items three through six.

"So those are the steps you will put into your drawing and your brain training story."

Deana added her observations. "Just so you know, now I have to stand there and tell Sara each step. Every day I have to stand there and remind her. If I don't, she just stops moving and gets caught up in her pretend play."

"So the routine that is in place now—where you are working harder than Sara—relies on you being an extension of Sara's brain. You are doing what the list will help her do: remember and plan each step in her morning routine." I continued. "Using the written list, and linking it to Sara's interests, changes your role. Now you will be able to coach Sara to check her list and to follow it. You can support her practicing to take care of herself."

"I see what you mean. That's definitely not how we used a checklist before. I can see how this will help Sara do more things on her own."

"Sara, I look forward to seeing your drawings and reading your story about getting yourself ready in the morning." I handed the checklist and chart to Sara. "Tell me two things about your new plan."

Sara took the paper and looked at the list. "Train my brain. Use my list."

"What are two things you got it of today's conversation so far, Deana?"

"That Sara can use her Pet Shop interest to become more self-sufficient." She paused. "And that maybe, finally, she can start to work harder and I can work less hard in the mornings."

"That's great. But remember, you two have been doing the same routine for 11 years. It will take time and practice for this new brain training routine to become as natural as the old routine is now."

"Sara, there is one other thing I would like to talk about today with you and your mother. I want to make a list with the two of you." I held the notepad and pencil and waited for Sara to respond.

Sara had resumed her place on the floor and had regrouped by focusing on her toys. "Okay."

I turned towards Deana. "I noticed earlier that when I asked about school, Sara told us the two things she did not like about going were 'too much work and too many people.' So I thought it might be a good idea to make a list of five things Sara's teachers need to know about her." I wrote: "5 things my teachers need to know about me" on the paper.

"Sara, can you tell me the end of this sentence? I learn best when . . ."

Sara repeated my sentence to start her answer. "I learn best when . . ." She was still focused on her play scenario and it was obvious that she was having difficulty shifting from her agenda to mine.

"Let's do some quick brain training right now!" I said. "Sara, you are enjoying playing out your scene right now and it is really hard for you to stop and talk with me. Let's try something different." I folded a piece of paper into a small square and wrote the word "pause" on it. Under the word I drew two parallel lines; the symbol for pausing a video.

"Here is our 'pause' button. When I hand the button to you that is your sign to push your pause button in your play scene and to get ready to answer one question. Are you ready to try it?"

Sara nodded. I handed her the pause button.

I asked her: "Ready? On pause?" Sara sat attentively and I provided the sentence prompt again: "I learn best when . . ."

Sara held the paper. "I learn best when there aren't too many people around."

"Great! Now hand the pause button back to me and continue with your scene."

Sara handed the paper back to me and resumed her play. I wrote down her response.

After a minute of play I prepared her for another pause event. "Sara, here comes the pause button again."

She reached out and held it. "Ready? On pause?" She nodded. "Tell me if this sentence is true about you: Too much talking and too much listening are hard work for me."

Sara nodded vigorously. "I don't like it when the teacher talks a lot."

"How about when she shows you what you are supposed to do?"

"I like that."

I reached out and Sara handed the pause button back to me. We continued this routine until we completed the list of five items.

When we were finished, I asked Sara to read the list to her mother.

"Five things my teacher needs to know about me. By Sara. Number one: I learn best when I'm in a small group without too many classmates. Number two: Noise and movement in the classroom bother me and make it hard for me to concentrate. Number three: Too much talking and too much listening is hard work for me and I do better when my teacher shows me what to do. Number four: I like to see things and learn by watching and seeing better than just by listening. And number five: I learn best when I can take short breaks to recharge my battery."

Deana looked at her daughter with an expression of positive regard as she listened to Sara read her list. "You did a great job with that, Sara. I am so proud of you. I know your teachers will appreciate hearing about what you need from them to do your best."

Sara stood close to her mother's side and handed her the paper. Her mother reached out and gave Sara a sideways hug.

"Great job, Sara." I added. "Sara, you did some excellent work in here today. Maybe you and your mother could get a special binder or notebook to keep your collection of stories about yourself. You like to collect things so now in addition to collecting Littlest Pet Shop toys and information you can start collecting information about Sara at age 11. Here is the pause button to add to your collection. Be sure to practice using this at home with your mom."

Deana smiled. "I like that. Let's start our collection of Sara information. We can stop and pick out a binder on our way home."

Sara agreed. "A Littlest Pet Shop binder!"

Shaping the Narrative Shift from Prompt-Dependence to Autonomy

Now let's discuss the therapy conversation with Sara and her mother from the narrative point of view. When the session began, Sara was aloof and disengaged with the conversational process. Her mother described being trapped in a negative morning routine with no end in sight. As the session progressed, Sara became increasingly more engaged in the problem-solving process. Her mother was able to experience a discussion of this difficult topic while working less hard than her daughter during the session. Both Sara and her mother left the session with concrete ways to begin the shift from prompt-dependence to autonomy.

What specific narrative tools were used in this session to support the shift from prompt-dependence to autonomy?

- To engage Sara in the conversation, a two-step process was used. First, by using her name and telling her that I would be asking her a question, I gave her time to inhibit her play and to practice flexible thinking. Then I gave her binary choices. This allowed her to use her working memory to organize her response. It also established a routine of limited required responses. This predictable routine helped Sara regulate her anxiety that was triggered by incoming language and social demands. Examples of the use of binary structure during the session include asking Sara to *"Tell me two things about your new plan,"* and *"Tell me if this sentence is true about you; Too much talking and too much listening are hard work for me."*
- Sara's maladaptive morning routine was externalized and rendered neutral when it was defined as "hard work." The contrast between where Deana was working harder (Sara's morning routine) and where Sara was working harder (at school) was highlighted. Sara was enlisted to help her mother solve the dilemma (*"So maybe your mom needs your help figuring out how you can get started in the mornings a little more on your own"*), allowing for the introduction of the age-appropriate shift from mother to daughter in owning the need for a change in the morning routine. Both mother and daughter experienced the shift from prompt-dependence to autonomy during the session.
- Documents were used to support the shift from prompt-dependence to autonomy. The documents were structured as binary contrast sheets, and lists. This binary, structured approach helped Sara identify the shift from "Mom help now" to "Help myself." The six steps in her morning routine were placed on the list in the "Help myself" column. Later in the session, the use of the "Five things my teacher needs to know about me" list provided a document that was part of Sara's developing sense of autonomy and self-advocacy.
- The concept of "brain training" provided Sara and her mother with a concrete way to conceptualize the learning process for Sara. Autonomy is powerfully embedded in the narrative of "brain training." Deana was able to move from providing the step-by-step

prompting for her daughter and move into the role of facilitating Sara's increased autonomy (*"Now you will be able to coach Sara to check her list and to follow it. You can support her practicing to take care of herself."*).

- The concept of "brain training" was linked to Sara's area of preferred interest. Sara demonstrated a fluid routine for acting out scenes with her Littlest Pet Shop figurines. This was used as an entry point to link an existing area of autonomy with her deficit area of initiating and completing her morning routine. This link was reinforced through the suggestion that Sara use her drawing skills to create a visual scenario regarding her morning routine as a form of checklist or step-by-step map.

- The operationalization of her independent enactment of her morning routine as an extension of her sensory-focused play was specifically intended to set up a goal-directed routine. Specifically, by associating the morning routine with the actions of her preferred Littlest Pet Shop character, Blythe Baxter, Sara was more likely to initiate this goal-directed routine.

- The visual, externalized process of using the "pause button" allowed Sara and her mother to experience a way to practice building cognitive flexibility for Sara. The use of a concrete object that Sara could hold while "pausing" and shifting from her agenda to mine provided a powerful way for Sara to experience autonomy in a conversation. This was in direct contrast to the resistance and anxiety she routinely experienced when demands were placed on her to shift her focus from her preferred activity to the "hard work" of participating in a verbal conversation. The use of the object clearly signaled the incoming demand.

- The self-advocacy list ("Five things my teacher needs to know about me") was introduced to help Sara begin to develop an autonomy narrative. Having Sara read her list allowed her and her mother to share an experience that radiated autonomy. This was in sharp contrast to their routine interactions.

- Self-advocacy and autonomy were supported in this session when the notion of starting a collection in the form of a binder to store her stories about herself was introduced (*"You like to collect things so now in addition to collecting Littlest Pet Shop toys and information you can start collecting information about Sara at age 11."*).

- Resiliency was introduced by predicting the likelihood that fluctuations and inconstancy would be an inherent part of the skills acquisition process. (*"But remember, you two have been doing the same routine for 11 years. It will take time and practice for this new brain training routine to become as natural as the old routine is now."*).

Notes

1 Baddeley, Alan (2007). *Working Memory, Thought, and Action*. Oxford, England: Oxford University Press.
2 Barkley, Russell A. (2012). *Executive Functions: What They Are, How They Work, and Why They Evolved*. New York, NY: Guilford Press.
3 Cooper-Kahn, Joyce, and Dietzel, Laurie (2008). *Late, Lost, and Unprepared: A Parents' Guide to Helping Children with Executive Functioning*. Bethesda, MD: Woodbine Press.
4 Hill, Elisabeth L., and Frith, Uta (2003). "Understanding Autism: Insights from Mind and Brain." *Philosophical Transactions Royal Society of London B*, Volume 358, pages 281–289.

6 Disorder to Style

Start the Conversation about Style

- Shift the focus of the family narrative through the reframe from disorder to style.
- Frame autism spectrum differences as the individual's style of interacting and managing in the world.
- Highlight the role of adaptive sensory routines.

A Place for Disorder and a Place for Style

- The language of disorders and disabilities is an integral part of medical care and determines access to services.
- Many school services and supports can only be accessed after a disability has been identified.
- Maintaining the language of disorders and disabilities within the family system includes negative connotations and limits the development of skills and autonomy.

Identifying and Managing Autism Spectrum Differences

- Help individuals and their families develop a narrative that focuses on identifying and managing autism spectrum differences.
- Build a story arc from examples of successful interactions and coping skills and place development in the context of neuro-typical development.
- Deficits can be framed as brain style differences that require strategies and "brain training."

From Disorder to Style

The diagnosis of Autism Spectrum Disorder sets a lifelong process in motion for individuals and their families. What role do autism spectrum differences play in the identity of the child, adolescent, or young adult with the diagnosis? How does this diagnosis fit into a life story?

Clinicians working with children and their families support the development of individual life stories when they frame autism spectrum differences as the individual's style of interacting and managing in the world. When you introduce the framework of style (thinking style, brain style) in your work with families, the narrative focus shifts from disorder to style. This shift is important. The language of disorders and disabilities is an integral part of medical care and determines access to services. Many school services and supports can only be accessed after a disability has been identified. The language of disorders and disabilities is part of the story.

When families integrate the language of diagnostic labels into the family system, the process, by definition, includes negative connotations. In the therapy context, starting the conversation about style helps families construct a narrative that emphasizes their unique situation. The conversation about style allows individuals and their families to build a story arc from examples of successful interactions and coping skills rather than emphasizing deficits. Deficits can be framed as brain style differences that require strategies and "brain training."

Starting the Conversation about Style with Nestor and His Parents

Nestor, a 19-year-old young man who was once again living at home after an unsuccessful first semester at college, walked into my office with his parents, Sophia and Spencer. Both of his parents were smartly dressed and entered the room with determination and purpose. Nestor was casually dressed and appeared mildly disheveled. His shoulders were hunched and his face was arranged in a mild grimace. After a cursory nod in my direction and a mumbled greeting he made a direct approach to a chair and slumped into it.

I had met with Nestor several times prior to this session with his parents. His mother contacted me when Nestor returned home, requesting therapy for Nestor and for the family. My initial sessions with Nestor allowed him to talk about himself without his parents. In our sessions Nestor presented a profile of a complex and multilayered young adult. He was academically gifted and excelled in the areas of math, science, and computer technology. Nestor was an avid gamer and had a particular interest in massively multiplayer online games from Southeast Asia. He maintained active relationships with his gaming counterparts all over the world.

Nestor was experiencing significant depression and anxiety about failing out of college. His narrative in our first session centered on his identity as a failure. He linked this failure identity to his "autism and ADHD." Although Nestor was gifted academically he struggled to maintain his hygiene, regulate his sleeping habits, and meet deadlines. He had secured a part-time job in a warehouse since returning home. Although he depended on his mother to get him out of bed on the days he had to go to work, Nestor was a reliable and pleasant employee. When his employer learned about Nestor's math skills he added some bookkeeping duties to his job.

In our sessions Nestor and I talked about what it meant when he referred to his "autism and ADHD." We started the conversation about his brain style. Nestor was able to reframe his identity from the static identity as the person with "autism and ADHD" to his identity of a young man with a unique brain style. The key brain style differences highlighted in our sessions included understanding the function of his gaming. Gaming for Nestor, especially during this phase of his life when he was in transition, served the function of regulating his anxiety about the uncertainty of his current circumstances. He was able to identify that gaming also blocked out his unpleasant emotions regarding his school failure. Although Nestor was intellectually capable, the process of managing language and social interactions required a great deal of effort from him. It took energy. Gaming, and socializing with his gaming counterparts, was restorative and energizing. As we created this narrative about the function of gaming, Nestor was able to gain a sense of control over his emotional process. Understanding the function of gaming made logical sense to him. This added predictability to his uncertain circumstances. This in turn helped him use his restored energy after gaming to apply himself to the tasks he needed to accomplish to successfully transition back to college. Through our discussions about the function of his gaming, we characterized Nestor's brain style.

We also discussed Nestor's brain style differences in terms of his uneven development. Nestor was and always had been gifted in his academic abilities. This was in stark contrast to his lifelong challenges to manage daily functional routines. This discussion led Nestor to an understanding of his brain style differences; differences he could directly address and do something about. Strategies could be planned and implemented. These initial conversations about his brain style differences shifted Nestor from a position of being held captive by the immutable force of his "autism and ADHD" to one of empowerment. These conversations paved the way for Nestor to talk about himself with his parents in their joint session.

I also met with his parents, Sophia and Spencer, prior to the family session. They told their story. They sent Nestor off to college after he successfully completed high school with academic honors. It was a shock to them when he was unable to maintain this level of successful functioning when he was in the college setting. Since his return home, Sophia was in daily conflict with her son. She battled with him on all fronts. Sophia expressed deep concern that Nestor was addicted to video games and that he would never live up to his potential. Both of his parents worried that the combination of Nestor's autism, ADHD, and depression would result in his never leaving home or gaining independence. Sophia and Spencer interpreted their son's lack of transparency in his activities and his empty promises to take responsibility for his actions as dishonest and manipulative behavior. The family was mired in anger, frustration, and blaming. In our conversation I introduced the reframe that Nestor's returning home was a necessary reboot, or relaunching, phase essential for his transition from adolescence to young adult life. We discussed his transition in the context of neuro-typical development. All young people and their families go through some stress as the transformation from teenager to young adult takes place. In Nestor's case, the abrupt transition from the supports provided by his mother in all areas except academic content (organization of his materials and management of his daily life details) to the autonomy required in college resulted in his inability to manage on his own.

Introducing the reframing from disorder to style was the first step in the sessions with Nestor and the separate session with his parents. Now it was time to help them make the shift as a family.

Sophia sat poised at the edge of her chair while Spencer sat back and crossed his legs with authority.

"So, Nestor, I'm glad we are having an opportunity for you to meet with your parents. You all have a lot to talk about." I started the session by addressing Nestor.

Sophia jumped in. "This morning is another good example of how bad things are right now. Nestor's gaming is out of control."

"That's all you ever talk about! You came into my room last night and threatened to take my computer. That is just not right!" Nestor sat up and shouted at his mother.

"Don't yell at your mother. She's just trying to help you," Spencer said.

"Well it's not helping! Threatening to take my computer is a violation of my civil rights!"

"And I will not have addictive gaming going on in my house!" Sophia retorted.

"Sophia, Nestor: I have a question," I interrupted the argument.

Both Nestor and Sophia turned to me, expectantly. "As I'm listening to the two of you, it struck me that this must be what it's like at home when this topic comes up. Tell me, you two: Does it ever feel like you're both doing the same thing, over and over again? Having the same argument over and over again?"

"Yes!" Sophia exclaimed. "It's the same thing every time and nothing ever changes!"

"Nestor? What do you think?" I prompted Nestor to contribute.

"It's like being stuck on a really bad game level."

"Even though it doesn't feel particularly good, or give either one of you the result that you want, the two of you are quite good at arguing with each other."

"We've certainly had a lot of practice, "Sophia said.

"Every day since I came home," Nestor added.

"Exactly. You have a routine that is familiar to all of you. Nestor retreats into his gaming world, you get activated and engage him in an argument, and Spencer interprets your intentions."

"Yeah, well it's not getting us anywhere," Sophia remarked.

"That's why we're here," Spencer said.

"So while you're here, we can begin talking about doing something different, instead of more of the same." Now that we had shifted from the familiar content of their argument, they were ready to try something different.

"Since I am just now getting to know your family, let's talk about what things were like last year, before Nestor graduated from high school. Sophia, I'm guessing you have worked very hard over the years to support and help your son manage the details that are part of daily life."

Sophia considered this for a moment. "I have worked hard to support my son. He's so smart and capable academically, but he's a mess when it comes to practical details. Between the autism and ADHD it's been a full time job keeping him on track."

"Both you and Nestor talk about 'the autism and ADHD.' Have you noticed that, Nestor? You and your mom have that in common."

"True. But where do you think I get that? She talks to me all the time about my autism and my ADHD. And now she's adding that I'm addicted to gaming. Which I'm *not*, by the way."

"So let's talk about a different way to think about your 'autism and ADHD.' Those are just labels. They don't really tell us much about you, do they?" I turned to his parents. "Nestor is really a remarkable young man. And the two of you have done a remarkable job helping him all these years. It's been a big blow to all of you that Nestor's first attempt to launch from the family resulted in the need to come home and reboot."

Sophia struggled with her emotions as she responded. "It's just that he was doing so well, you know? And he has so much potential."

Spencer added his thoughts. "We thought he was ready, he thought he was ready, but clearly he wasn't ready."

Nestor addressed his parents directly. "Don't you know that I feel like a failure? I was supposed to be ready. This wasn't supposed to happen." He crossed his arms. "And now it's exponentially worse because you're constantly telling me what a screw-up I am. Me and my 'autism and ADHD.'"

His parents looked at Nestor with focused attention while he spoke. Spencer replied first.

"Son, we don't see you as a screw-up. That's why we're here—to figure out how to help and support you."

Sophia added, "I know I sound like I'm telling you you're messing up, but that's because I'm so worried about you."

"Well you don't need to worry so much, Mom! You need to get a clue."

"So Nestor, let's help your parents understand things better from your perspective. Why don't you talk with them about how your view of your brain style has changed since we started our conversations." I prompted Nestor to use his own words to talk about his brain style differences with his parents.

Nestor gathered his thoughts before addressing his parents. "One of the things I've learned since coming in here is that there is nothing wrong with me. My brain works differently. It's not 'my autism and ADHD.' It's my style." He paused for a minute before adding, "And by the way, my brain isn't the only one with a style in this family."

Both of his parents smiled.

"You're so right about that," his mother said.

"So, Nestor, your mother brought up your gaming when you all came in here and labeled it as an addiction. Can you talk with her about how your gaming fits in with your brain style?" I prompted Nestor to change the conversation between him and his mother surrounding the topic of gaming.

Nestor nodded once before turning towards his mother. "Right now it looks like I'm gaming a lot, but what you don't know is that while I'm gaming, I can block out my bad feelings and negative thoughts about crashing and burning at school. I need that break from the bad stuff. Also what you don't know is that after I've done a bunch of gaming I'm using my computer to figure out what I need to do next to get back in school. So every time you see me on the computer, I'm not always gaming. Just so you know."

Sophia responded. "That makes sense. I can see how it blocks things out for you. That doesn't change the fact that I am worried that you are spending way too much time online."

"Everyone I know is at college, Mom. And even if I went out and saw someone I know, I would have to tell them I crashed and burned. When I'm online I feel good because everyone knows me and my team asks me for help and advice. I need that right now because literally everywhere else things are not good."

Spencer added his observation. "Nestor, when you tell us what you're thinking it helps us a lot. I can understand how you need to block things out sometimes. Do you think if we could be less upset with you that you might come out of your room more and spend some time talking with us? I'd like that."

"I'd like that too, Dad. But every time we talk, you and mom tell me that I'm a screw-up."

"That's because when I ask you if you've brushed your teeth or picked up your clothes or called the community college for information about enrolling, you tell me you've done it but you're lying." Sophia reverted to the familiar routine.

"Sophia, what do you think about Nestor's changing view that he is learning to understand and manage his brain style differences?" I asked.

"That's a good thing. But I'm still frustrated."

"Of course. You've been working very hard on your son's success. He's depended on you for years. Now he's figuring out how to manage his life details with a little less help. It's an adjustment for both of you."

"The problem is, if I back off, nothing gets done!" Sophia insisted.

"But it does get done, Mom! I have a job. I am getting ready to sign up for school." Nestor paused. "Okay, so I don't brush my teeth all the time."

"Thank you! Usually you tell me you've done things but you haven't." Sophia sighed. "Nestor, I know you're trying, and I see your progress. And I like the idea that you are taking responsibility and learning how to manage your differences."

I asked Sophia a question. "So, Sophia, would you like it if Nestor talked with you more openly about his plans and goals?"

"Of course!"

"So talk with him about that. Try to focus on moving forward and making a plan together."

Sophia nodded. "I'd like that very much, Nestor. How can we make it happen?"

Nestor looked at his mother. "You are a big help, you know that, right? Just stop being on my case all the time. I need my gaming time. I am doing my job and checking out the school schedule for next semester. Once I get through the next semester and bring up my GPA, I plan to apply to the engineering department at a four-year school." He squinted his eyes and extended his head towards his mother. "See? I have goals."

"Nestor, it's so good to hear you tell us these details. And I want to help you, not drive you away." They looked at each other and shared a moment without conflict.

His father held up a hand with his palm towards his son. Nestor reached out and they slapped palms.

"You can use this time you have together while Nestor is rebooting to help him develop the routines he needs to manage his brain style differences as he gets ready to leave home and go to college again." I turned to Nestor. "You are figuring things out, and I will continue to help you understand and manage your brain style. But you could also still use their help, right?"

"Right."

"So how can you and your mom, and you and your dad, work together in a way that feels better for all of you?"

Spencer took the lead in this part of the conversation. "Nestor, how about meeting me for lunch once a week? You seem to relax and talk more over a meal. If you check your work schedule and get it to me I can arrange a day to meet you for lunch."

"I could do that," Nestor said.

Spencer continued. "But remember that you are going to have to take responsibility to let me know your schedule. That's the only way this will work."

"Wait, could you remind me on Sunday nights? I get my weekly schedule then but you know it's hard for me to remember to do things."

"That will work," Spencer agreed.

Sophia entered the conversation. "Okay, it sounds like arranging a time is something that will work better for you than having me spontaneously reminding you or asking you to do something. Can we agree on a time to meet? That way I know I'll have a specific time to go over details and questions with you. I'll have to work on waiting until our set time but that will probably be good for *my* brain style."

"Maybe we could meet in the kitchen after dinner. But let's make it a short meeting. When you ask too many questions I get overloaded," Nestor said.

"I can see that now. I can always make a list. That would let you see what's on my mind that we need to discuss."

"Good idea, Mom." Nestor raised his eyebrows. "One more thing, Mom. I don't want you coming into my room and threatening to take away my computer. I'm not a little kid anymore."

"I can respect that, but Nestor, if you really understand that you're not a little kid anymore, then you can understand that it's important for you to practice daily habits of getting regular sleep, brushing your teeth, wearing clean clothes, and getting yourself out of bed in time to get to work. Those are the things that got you into trouble at college."

"You're right, Mom. But I still need your help to remind me to do those things."

I entered the conversation. "The more you practice those routines the more your brain learns to anticipate the routines as part of your daily life, Nestor." I turned to Sophia and Spencer. "It would probably be helpful for you and Nestor to work together in here on the project of helping Nestor develop these independent brain routines. What are your thoughts about coming in here to work on that?"

Sophia nodded her agreement. "Nestor has talked more with me in here today than in the past two months since he's been home."

"This is what we've been needing. I'm on board," Spencer added.

"What do you think, Nestor?" I asked.

"Yup. Let's do that."

Shaping the Narrative Shift from Disorder to Style

Now let's discuss the therapy process with Nestor and his parents from the narrative point of view. When the family session began, Sophia was agitated and confrontational, Spencer was passive, and Nestor was intractable. Each had a role in the well-established family routine. Although all of them were willing to change, none of them had found a way to break through the inflexible pattern to move the process forward.

What specific narrative tools were used in this family session to support the shift from disorder to style?

- Prior to setting up the family session, I scheduled several individual sessions with Nestor. Structurally, this signaled to the family that Nestor was a young adult who was separate from his parents. It allowed Nestor to begin the process of crafting his individual identity and narrative separate from the well-entrenched family narrative.
- Prior to setting up the family session, I scheduled a session with Sophia and Spencer. Structurally, this emphasized their role as a couple and as parents. They needed to tell their stories and I needed to listen. The common language of Nestor's *"autism and ADHD"* surfaced in the stories told by both Nestor and his parents.
- In Nestor's individual sessions, the shift from his externalization of his *"autism and ADHD"* to an understanding of his brain style moved him from his static relationship with his differences to a dynamic one. When he gained an understanding of the adaptive function of his sensory routine (gaming) he gained power and autonomy. He also gained the necessary language to change the conversation with his mother, who was framing his gaming as an addiction.
- During the family session, members enacted their familiar roles. Commenting on the arguing process between Nestor and Sophia shifted the conversation from the familiar routine of focusing on the content (*"Threatening to take my computer is a violation of my civil rights!"* and *"And I will not have addictive gaming going on in my house!"*) to the process (*"Does it ever feel like you're both doing the same thing, over and over again? Having the same argument over and over again?"*). This process observation shifted the conversation to the key issue for Sophia behind the repetitive arguing routine (*"Sophia, I'm guessing you have worked very hard over the years to support and help your son manage the details that are part of daily life."*). Overtly recognizing Sophia's efforts allowed the family to talk about Nestor's competencies as well as the family anguish over his recent failure to launch to college.
- During the family session, encouraging Nestor to share his perspective on gaming with his parents helped shift the family from conflict to supportive alliance. Rather than remaining focused on convincing her son that he had an addiction, Sophia was able to hear the work her son was doing and to suggest ways she could be helpful (*"Nestor, I know you're trying and I see your progress"*; *"I'd like that very much, Nestor. How can we make that happen?"*).

- Shifting the narrative between Sophia and Nestor allowed Spencer to take a more active role in mentoring his son (*"Nestor, how about meeting me for lunch once a week?"*). He modeled encouraging his son to engage in age-appropriate management of this arrangement (*"But remember that you are going to have to take responsibility to let me know your schedule. That's the only way this will work."*) and negotiated with his son when Nestor asked for a reminder (*"That will work."*).
- Nestor and his parents were caught in the narrative that he had failed and "crashed and burned" when he returned home after his first semester away. The metaphor of *"rebooting"* fit in with this family's focus on Nestor's computer use. It provided a neutral way to understand the relaunching process.
- Sophia needed a new role to support and help her son gain the necessary skills to take care of himself and live independently as an adult. The narrative of Nestor's brain style provided a way to reshape his mother's role from direct provider and prompter to that of his mentor and coach (*"You can use this time together while Nestor is rebooting to help him develop the routines he needs to manage his brain style differences as he gets ready to leave home and go to college again."*).
- Ending the family session with a plan for continued individual work with Nestor along with family work for the three of them allowed for a moment of consensus between Nestor and his parents. Instead of conflict, his parents were aligned with him in their commitment to support their son in his development of crucial life skills.

Section III

Narrative Development Across the Life Cycle

7 Young Children

Shaping the Family Story

- Providing facts and information about Autism Spectrum Disorder helps parents understand their child's diagnosis.
- Developing their child's individualized autism spectrum profile helps parents understand the diagnosis in a meaningful and individualized context.
- Your support helps parents manage the emotional impact of the diagnosis.

Linking Practical Supports to the Emerging Family Story

- Parents gain an understanding of the importance of visual supports when they understand their child's brain style differences.
- Communication supports, social supports, and sensory supports can be introduced through the entry point of the child's individualized autism spectrum Brain Style Profile.
- The visual communication, social, and sensory supports gain personal meaning for parents when they are introduced in the individualized context.

Practicing Skills in the Therapy Setting

- Modeling skills with the young child helps parents gain skills.
- Practicing their skills with their child in the therapy context helps parents gain confidence.
- Providing education about autism spectrum differences and resources helps parents reduce their anxiety.

All families with young children experience significant stress as the concept of "parent" collides with the reality of daily life with an infant, toddler, or preschool child. The very nature of parenting young children includes daily contradictions and uncertainties. For parents of children with autism spectrum differences, this ambivalence is magnified.

Parents of young children with autism spectrum differences often describe the experience of realizing that their child is developing with differences as a growing sense of concern. This concern can range from worry that comes and goes, to a strong sense of anxiety about the child's differences, to a sense of dread about what it might mean if the child does not develop speech, social play, or cope with routine events. Many parents go through a process of watching their child in comparison to other young children, noticing with dismay when their child appears aloof, or plays with objects in the same way over and over, or doesn't seem to look at people or respond to social smiles. It can be confusing for parents when their child *does* behave like other children at times. What does it mean if their child cuddles and seeks out hugs sometimes but keeps people at arm's length at other times? If their child shows an early passion for letters and numbers, and excels at manipulating electronic devices, parents often struggle with whether that should be looked at as a good thing or something to worry about. Sometimes one parent expresses concerns while their partner dismisses those anxieties.

When the diagnosis of Autism Spectrum Disorder enters the family story it can be a stressful and confusing time. What does it mean, exactly, when a pediatrician, psychologist, or other professional uses that term? Many parents report a cascading effect when they hear the formal diagnosis for their child. Questions about practical details come up. Does this diagnosis affect whether or not their child will be able to go to college, drive a car, get married, get a job? In other words, most parents of young children experience a process of feeling enclosed by limitations when they hear the term "autism."

Clinicians working with parents and their young children with autism spectrum differences provide timely and crucial support when they guide the parents through the process of shaping the singular family story. Parents benefit from gaining a global understanding of the diagnosis. This includes learning factual information about autism spectrum differences, as becoming informed contributes to the shift from powerless to capable. When you share factual information about the autism spectrum with parents of a young child, and pair this with the ability to engage the young child in play with sensory materials, parents gain confidence in your ability to deal effectively with their family story. Your support helps them manage the emotional impact of this sometimes frightening and bewildering diagnostic process.[1]

So what goes into shaping the family story when a young child has received the diagnosis of Autism Spectrum Disorder? Shaping the language the parents use when describing their child, and developing a document that lays out the child's individualized autism spectrum profile, is a key part of this process. This document helps parents understand their child's diagnosis in a meaningful and individualized context.

Understanding the child's brain style is important and it provides the entry point to teach parents about practical supports that are a good fit for the child's autism spectrum brain style differences. The descriptive triangle framework helps parents link practical supports to the emerging family story in a meaningful way. Visual communication supports, social supports, and sensory supports can be readily discussed within the context of the child's profile in these three key areas. With parents and their young child present in the therapy setting, you are able to incorporate modeling, practice, and education into your sessions. Parents gain competence and confidence and children gain skills and a sense of control and predictability as the family story emerges.

Rusty's Parents Develop Their Story

Rusty, a sturdily built toddler who had just passed his third birthday, filled the room with his exuberant, positive energy. His world was comprehensively and enthusiastically organized around trains. When I met Rusty, he wore a Thomas the Tank Engine shirt and strode into my office hugging a Thomas the Tank Engine backpack to his chest. His mother, Jennifer, had alerted me during our phone conversation that Rusty had just received a diagnosis of Autism Spectrum Disorder, and that he loved trains. This was the first session for Rusty, his mother Jennifer, and his father, Randy.

When Rusty entered the room his gaze fell on a strategically placed pair of blocks. Each block, or cube, displayed a graphic of half of a vehicle. The two blocks fit together to make the sound of the vehicle when placed together. The cube to the left facing Rusty contained a picture of the front half of a train engine while the cube to the right had a picture of the back half.

"Train!" Rusty exclaimed as he walked towards the cubes.

"Train!" I mirrored, as I placed my hands on the sides of the train cube and gently pushed them towards each other. Rusty picked up on my visual cue and took over. He pushed the cubes together and when they connected, the blocks emitted the sound of a train engine blowing smoke.

Rusty erupted in a delightful, spontaneous laugh. I laughed along with him and both of his parents smiled. I exchanged glances and smiles with Jennifer and Randy. Rusty's gaze, however, remained firmly fixed on the cubes and the cause-and-effect sound created as he pushed the cubes together time and again. I turned one of the cubes to another side and the image of the front half of a helicopter appeared.

"Helicopter!" I said. I tapped the second cube. "Find the helicopter."

Rusty pleasantly but firmly repositioned the cube so that the front of the train was facing him. "Train!" He continued his routine. After a few more repetitions, Rusty initiated rotating the cube back to the helicopter.

"Helicopter!" He enthusiastically labeled it.

"Helicopter!" I mirrored. "Like Harold!" Harold is the name of the helicopter in the Thomas the Tank Engine world.

Rusty immediately looked at me and took in my presence for the first time when he heard this familiar name. "Harold and Thomas!" Rusty stood in front of me and looked at me, clearly prompting me to pursue this line of conversation.

"Thomas is engine number . . . ," I said.

"One!" Again Rusty looked at me.

"Thomas is the color . . . ," I prompted.

"Blue!" Rusty erupted in his contagious laughter once again, turned the blocks back to the train image and pushed them together several more times.

Unfortunately my Thomas the Tank Engine repertoire was nearing its end, as I could not recall the names of any of the other trains. This did not put a damper of Rusty's enthusiasm for the topic.

"Percy!" he exclaimed.

That was my cue to continue the conversation. "Percy is engine number . . ."

"Six!"

"Percy is the color . . ."

"Green!"

Thanks to Rusty's extensive labeling abilities, we were able to have a spirited conversation about his favorite topic. However, when I showed Rusty interesting toys that were not train-related and when I used language to label anything other than trains, he moved away from me and unzipped his backpack, taking out several trains and hooking them together. He lay on the floor and placed his head in a direct line with his linked trains. He quietly rolled the trains back and forth, closely examining the visual details. His parents and I were silent as we watched Rusty retreat to his nonverbal world of exploring his familiar trains.

I blew some bubbles and they drifted into Rusty's line of vision. This activated him and he jumped up. "Bubbles!"

I continued to blow bubbles and Rusty approached me, popping bubbles and laughing. When he was back in close proximity to me I handed him a puzzle piece that fit into a square wooden inset board. This puzzle had pieces shaped like fish. Rusty stood and concentrated as he scanned the inset shapes, searching for the match with the seahorse he was holding. I tapped the correct inset and said: "Seahorse." Rusty placed the piece in the correct place. I handed him an octopus and waited a beat before tapping the octopus spot on the puzzle.

"Octopus!" Rusty correctly named the piece as he placed it in the puzzle.

Just as he had comfortably fallen into a routine with our train conversation, Rusty fell into the routine of receiving a puzzle piece, naming it or hearing the name, and placing the piece into the wooden board. After he placed the last piece I handed Rusty a wooden fishing pole with a magnet attached to the end. Each fish piece contained a metal knob that allowed Rusty to lift the pieces out of the puzzle with the fishing pole. He immediately understood this routine and concentrated on getting the magnet from the end of the fishing pole to connect with a fish piece. I took the plastic zip-up bag that I used to store the puzzle pieces and formed it into a fish-eating bag. I grasped each side of the bag and made the opening open and close repeatedly while using an exaggerated voice to "speak" as the bag.

"Feed me! I'm hungry!"

Rusty alerted by stiffening his entire body as he guided the fish towards the bag. I helped him by having the bag gobble up the fish.

"Delicious! More fish!"

As we were establishing yet another predictable routine, Rusty burst out in his signature laugh and obeyed the bag's command. I added a language prompt, coaching Rusty to tell the bag: "open wide." After one prompt he was able to give the bag that command. When Rusty tried to place the fourth piece into the bag I changed the routine, adding an element of unpredictability.

"Uh!" The bag said. "Yucky!" I pushed the fish out of the opening of the bag and it flew in an arc and fell on the floor.

A look of concern covered Rusty's face with this new development. He hesitated, picked up the fish, and placed it back into the puzzle board. He selected a different piece and resumed the original routine.

As the fish hovered close to the bag's mouth, I asked Rusty a question. "Do you want the bag to eat it or spit it out?"

Rusty promptly replied in no uncertain terms. "Eat it."

The bag followed his command. Each time I asked Rusty his preference he asserted that the bag needed to eat the fish. When he placed the last fish into the bag I prompted him to place the fishing pole in as well and to zip up the bag and drop it into the large mesh bag I held in front of him. Rusty released the bag of fish into the container and moved away to resume his solitary play with his trains. We continued this pattern of work (activities directed by me) and play (self-directed activities) while his parents, Jennifer and Randy, watched closely. Each time he completed an activity with me I prompted Rusty to drop the materials into the mesh bag.

After Rusty had completed several inset puzzles with me and had shown anticipation of and follow through with the routine of "start to finish" I handed Rusty a puzzle that required color matching.

"Give this to Mommy," I said.

Rusty stood for a moment, taking in this new direction. Then he took the puzzle board to his mother. I handed her the bag containing the pieces. "Your turn to play," I said.

Jennifer took the bag with the pieces and handed Rusty one piece at a time while he leaned over the puzzle board and concentrated on the visual matching. She prompted him to verbally label the colors, modeled the labeling, and used the mesh bag clean up routine.

As Jennifer practiced the routine with Rusty I took out a Velcro ball and two Velcro mitts and held them until they were finished. I looked at Randy. "Now it's your turn." I smiled and so did Randy. I handed Randy the two mitts and the attached ball.

Randy held up one of the mitts and held it out towards his son. He helped Rusty hold the strap on the back of the mitt and then showed him how to take the ball off and throw it so it stuck to the mitt. Rusty was immediately intrigued with the process of pulling the ball off the Velcro and smashing it back on the front of his mitt. However, with some excellent prompting by his father, he was able to successfully throw and catch the ball several times. It was clear that he was done with the activity after two exchanges and Randy responded by holding up the mesh bag and dropping his mitt into it. His son promptly followed the visual prompt, dropping his mitt with the ball attached to it into the mesh bag. He then retreated to a far corner of the room for some regrouping time with his trains.

As Rusty settled into his comfort zone of solitary train play, I turned to Jennifer and Randy.

"Rusty is a delightful boy. Tell me your thoughts about how he has been in here so far today." I prompted his parents to process their experience.

Randy started the conversation. "He handled this new situation a lot better than I thought he would. I thought he would do what he usually does, which is stick to his trains and to himself." He looked thoughtfully at his son before turning back to me. "He really came out of his train world today. That was good for us to see. I enjoyed playing catch with him. Having that bag routine was good. Usually when I try to get him to play catch with me he wanders off."

Jennifer agreed. "I was happy that you got to see the difference between when Rusty is on his own and when you try to get him to try new things." She paused before continuing. "I noticed that you had him put everything into bags, and zip up the bags, and drop them into the big bag every time you got to the end of an activity. He really did well with that. I was glad you had me practice doing the routine too instead of just watching."

"You both work so well with your son. And clearly he is comfortable with you so I'm glad practicing the clean-up routine was helpful. With all of these activities in here today Rusty was showing us how he thinks and how he organizes in the world. How his brain works, or his brain style." I paused for a moment to give time for his parents to absorb this wording. "Rusty creates and follows predictable routines. And he is able to generalize this love of routines to activities that do not involve his wonderful trains."

Jennifer applied this idea. "Like when he fed the bag the fish puzzle pieces—he was thrown off when you changed the routine. We thought it was funny but Rusty didn't like it. He went back to what he was doing before."

Randy said, "Rusty does love creating routines. I thought it was something we needed to change about him, especially after he got his diagnosis. I read about how obsessed some of these kids get with their stuff and we don't want to create a monster. We've thought about taking away his trains but you can see how much he loves them. They really bring him joy." Randy paused and swallowed before he continued. "He's such a happy little guy, you know? We love that about him."

"Rusty is clearly such a happy little boy. He has such a delightful way about him and his passion for trains is contagious. I can see how much you love him and appreciate him."

Both of his parents smiled.

"So let's talk about Rusty's passion for all things train-related. Instead of thinking of this interest as an obsession, let's look at what it does for him. Remember when he got me into a conversational loop about Thomas and friends? He was showing us that the visual predictability of his beloved trains helps him link up with language concepts. He was able to tell me the names of the trains, their colors, and their numbers. It was as if he could see them as he went through the list."

"Right, right, so true." Jennifer nodded in agreement.

"So the visual aspect of his trains tells us that Rusty is a child who organizes his thinking around visual input. We could say that he is a visual learner, as opposed to a learner who organizes around spoken language."

"Very much so," Randy agreed.

"So let's write down the brain style we see with Rusty as we talk about his style in detail. Let's start with how he is using his language and communication." I wrote "language and communication" at the top of the page. "Let's start with his strengths and then discuss some of his key differences."

I underlined the word "strengths."

"Because Rusty is a visual learner, he is developing an ever increasing vocabulary for labeling things that he sees, right?" I asked.

Jennifer and Randy nodded in agreement. "Every day he comes up with new words. His vocabulary is really exploding. But it's hard to get him to answer our questions," Jennifer explained.

"That's an important point. There is a big difference for your son between seeing an object or thinking about an object and remembering what it looks like and generating the words linked to that visual, and his ability to process incoming language. Most of the time incoming language doesn't come with visual cues, especially when your brain resists looking at people like Rusty's brain does. That makes incoming language a source of stress, and Rusty backs away from the source of that stress. Does that make sense?"

Randy spoke up this time. "That is how it is with him. If he decides to talk about something he does but he resists it when we start it."

"So a strength for Rusty in the area of language and communication is his ability to organize and use his language with visual contextual cues. That means if he can see it and make a visual association he is able to retrieve his language." I wrote: "ever increasing vocabulary for labeling" and "organizes, retrieves, and uses language best with visual contextual cues."

"Let's talk about a few more areas of strength for Rusty. Does he use his language to make requests of you? To ask for help?" I asked.

"He does both of those and is doing it more consistently since he turned three," Jennifer agreed. I wrote down "using his language consistently to make requests" and "asks for help."

"Once Rusty learns something—a new word or concept—does he hold on to it?"

"Yes, he never forgets anything he's learned."

I wrote: "learns and retains information well."

"And an area of difference for Rusty is his low threshold for incoming language demands. Would you agree?"

"That's him," Jennifer said.

"And when he uses language, it seems that he is mostly the one who starts it. The content of what he talks about is mostly labeling instead of social communication, or social commenting, correct?" I asked

"That's him," Randy said.

I wrote: "language use primarily self-initiated and focused on labeling instead of social communication."

"And I noticed that Rusty used a somewhat scripted style of speaking and spoke almost exclusively with an exclamatory, loud voice. Do you see that as well?" I asked.

"He is loud and enthusiastic when he talks. Or he's completely quiet, one or the other," Jennifer said.

"Another difference in Rusty's language is that he is not yet using shared, or social, language. In other words, he isn't quite able to have a back-and-forth exchange with you unless it is part of a routine, like naming the trains," I added.

I wrote: "not yet using shared, social language" and "uses a somewhat scripted style of speaking (exclamatory, loud)."

"Does that describe Rusty's language and communication style?" I asked.

"Definitely." Randy spoke for both of them as they nodded in agreement.

I started a second sheet, writing the words "social relationships and emotions" at the top.

"Now let's talk about Rusty's strengths and differences in the areas of social relationships and emotions. Let's start with social relationships." I wrote "strengths" and underlined it.

"Well, he's definitely a loving, enthusiastic, and happy boy," Jennifer said.

"And he has the best laugh in the world," Randy added.

"So true," I agreed. I wrote these descriptors down.

"There is another strength I noticed with Rusty and that was how he regulates or handles himself when the demands are too much for him. Instead of becoming upset or agitated he retreats into his solitary play and the wonderful world of his trains," I said.

His parents agreed. I wrote: "manages social stress by retreating into solitary play instead of becoming agitated or upset."

"And Rusty is beginning to show some brief, shared enjoyment when others share in his interests, right?" I asked.

"Right, we see that. He's making nice connections with us around his trains. He loves his track and takes me by the hand when I get home so I'll sit and watch him while he runs the trains. He's pretty good about saying 'look' when he wants my attention. Also, he's really good at fixing his trains when they jump the track or the pieces need to be put back together." Randy described their father-son shared activity.

I wrote: "starting to show shared enjoyment with preferred activities."

"Now let's discuss some of Rusty's differences in his social relationships. I noticed that Rusty's brain doesn't naturally register, or use, simple social cues like eye contact, changes in his facial expression, and so on," I said. "Am I describing what you experience with him?"

Jennifer nodded. "It's hard to get his attention. Every once in a while he takes my face in his hands and points it towards what he wants. But most of the time he avoids looking at us. He doesn't always follow where we're pointing. He does better when I use an exaggerated voice and facial expressions. Sort of like you did when you were making the bag eat the fish."

I wrote: "difficulty noticing, responding to, and using simple social cues" and "responds best to exaggerated voice and facial expressions."

"And just like with language demands, Rusty withdraws from the source of social demands. It's hard for him to participate in shared play," I said. His parents agreed and I wrote down the descriptive language.

"In the area of emotions, Rusty hasn't yet developed a vocabulary to express his emotions, has he?" I asked.

"No, we try to tell him happy, sad, mad, and show him the expressions but it's hard to get and keep his attention when we are showing him that," Jennifer recalled.

I wrote: "has not yet developed a labeling vocabulary to express his emotions."

"Does this sound like we're describing Rusty's style so far?" I asked.

"Yes."

"Absolutely."

"So let's talk about Rusty's style in the area of sensory use and interests." I wrote "sensory use and interests" on a third page. "Rusty showed some excellent strengths in this area. He has a strong memory for visual details and learns well with predictable visual routines, doesn't he?" I asked.

"That's a real strength for him. He learns quickly and doesn't forget things," Randy observed. I wrote: "strong memory for visual details," "learns well with predictable visual routines," and "learns quickly and retains information well."

"We already talked about this a little, but Rusty self-regulates with his trains. He sets up systematic, solitary routines with his beloved trains and that helps him regulate and regroup," I said. His parents agreed and I wrote: "self-regulates by engaging in self-directed activities with preferred materials."

"And I would say that Rusty is a visual thinker and a systematic thinker. Would you two agree?" I asked.

Jennifer looked thoughtful. "I have always thought that Rusty gets caught up in looking at things, but I hadn't really thought about it as the way he actually *thinks*. And he is systematic about things. So that fits. What do you think?" She turned to Randy.

"I think this is right on the mark. This sums up his world," Randy added.

I wrote the qualities "visual thinker" and "systematic thinker."

Randy continued to think about his son's world. "As far as differences go, Rusty likes to be in charge. He wants to do what he wants to do and it doesn't matter what we want him to do."

"That makes transition times challenging," I said, as I wrote: "Transition times can be difficult when he is engaged in a preferred activity."

Jennifer reflected on this point for a moment. "It's hard to get his attention away from his trains to follow directions."

"Have you noticed, Jennifer, that when you show Rusty while you give him direction that he does better?" I asked. "He's so visual in the way he organizes information that listening to directions can't compete with visual input, right?"

"So true," Jennifer agreed. I wrote: "requires visual cues paired with verbal requests to successfully transition from one activity to the next."

We reviewed the list of descriptors for Rusty in each of the three key areas, starting with strengths and moving on to differences.

Randy turned from the list and looked at me. "This really explains him. Up until now no one has been able to tell me what it means that my son has autism. And that is a troubling word, let me tell you. But this describes him."

"I'm glad this is helpful, Randy. Everyone has their own specific idea of what autism is when they hear the word. But it's a word, and Rusty is a wonderful, complex, and unique little boy. When we talk about his brain style, his profile, in this way, we are describing his autism spectrum differences. Those differences include some excellent strengths for Rusty. Understanding his strengths—and his differences—gives us the clues we need to develop the building blocks and supports to help him build a bridge from the way he organizes in the world to being able to go with the flow."

I added a fact about autism spectrum differences. "One in every 68 children shows this pattern of brain style differences. And each child who has these differences shows a unique profile within the same general pattern. Language and social interactions are harder work, while visual routines are regulating and organizing."

Randy nodded. He looked at Jennifer and she nodded as they shared a moment of reflection. "This explanation makes more sense than hearing that my child has autism. I don't want us to put any labels on him. But I know we need help to understand him and what he needs. I just want to learn how to help him."

"So the list we just made—Rusty's Brain Style Profile—gives us the clues we need to help him in the areas that are harder for him, like following your lead and tolerating interruptions in his play routines," I said. "Let's talk about ways to use his visual, systematic way of thinking to build a system to support Rusty's language and communication."

I continued. "Rusty loves all things related to trains, and he also sets up and follows predictable routines. Let's put those two things together in a visual schedule. You know that he organizes and retrieves his labeling language best with visual cues. So think about setting up a visual schedule for him that pairs pictures and words about each daily activity. Creating a visual schedule for Rusty that is in the form of a train track will naturally draw his attention to the schedule. Having the visual cues will allow you to pair verbal directions with visual cues, making it more likely that Rusty will attend to your words. Manipulating the train track schedule gives Rusty a transition activity or routine that is predictable and in his control."

Jennifer became visibly animated. "Rusty would love that! I can print out some pictures and make a schedule with a train track." She paused as she thought about the process. "I wonder if it would be best to have a small schedule that I could take to him throughout the day or if I should have a big one on his bedroom wall."

"Those are important details to consider, Jennifer. I think your first thought to have the schedule be portable is a good idea for Rusty. He will get the idea more quickly if the use of his schedule occurs as a natural part of each transition. A schedule the size of a sheet of paper would work well. You can laminate it after you come up with the train track graphic.

And you can use Velcro on the track schedule and on the cards so he can attach each card as he goes through his day."

"Yes, that would work. Maybe we could have a train depot on the back of his schedule where he can put the cards as he takes them off the track and finishes each event." Jennifer had a detailed plan already.

"Great idea, Jennifer. You and Rusty will have fun setting up his visual schedule. I'll give you a list of places online you can go to look at sample visual schedules. Then you can start using some visual supports with Rusty." I wrote down several web addresses so Jennifer and Randy could explore ideas after our session.

"Jennifer is really creative. And when she takes on a project it gets done." Randy said in support.

"I see that. You can start using visual communication supports to help Rusty anticipate transitions in his daily schedule with his overall schedule, but you can use visual supports for other things as well. For example, Rusty can be quite resistant to stopping what he is doing. Using a card that shows Rusty the sequence of 'first, then' would be very helpful for him." I drew a square on the page in front of me and added a t-shaped grid. Then I wrote "First" in the top left-hand box and "Then" in the top right-hand box. "You can add pictures to each box, visually signaling the sequence of 'first, then' for Rusty. He will begin to anticipate what he is being requested to do and anticipate that after he does a task for you he will have time for his trains or other preferred activity." I paused before continuing.

"Rusty would do well with pictures and written words underneath. You could use photos of actual objects or areas of the house to start with, but Rusty will be able to understand the pictures because he is already noticing visual details well. Having the words written underneath gives him opportunities to make the association between words and objects or events."

Jennifer and Randy nodded in agreement.

"He is already starting to recognize words in some of his books," Jennifer commented.

"You may also want to have duplicates of each picture so that you can hand the picture to Rusty while you tell him the upcoming event. Prompt Rusty by tapping the matching picture on the 'first, then' card to have him match the picture to the one on the card. You can use Velcro to allow Rusty to attach the matching picture to the card. The 'first, then' card can have a train motif as well."

"So it sounds like setting up the daily schedule and using the 'first, then' routine is something you are ready to set up for Rusty at home. There are a few more visual supports I'd like to suggest to help Rusty broaden his social and emotional understanding and vocabulary." I made the transition to addressing visual supports for the second area of the autism spectrum differences triangle.

"You mentioned that Rusty likes looking at books. Does he also like looking at photographs of family members?" I asked.

"He loves looking at photos. He finds them on my phone and almost seems to study them. He loves looking at his books too. That's part of our bedtime routine," Jennifer confirmed.

"Great. To help Rusty develop a vocabulary and understanding about himself and his world, I suggest putting together some books with photos of him and the people and events in his life. You can call them "Me and My Family" and "My Favorite Places" for example. Under each photo, write a brief caption in the first person, as if Rusty were speaking. You can make the books interactive by having him match the photos while you read the caption. Having these photo books available for Rusty to explore independently will help him practice the routine of seeing visual representations of social aspects of his life while labeling what he sees."

Randy nodded again. "I like that idea. Rusty needs our help in learning how to talk about the people in his life."

"So reading these interactive social books—these social stories—is something you can add to his routine. Be sure to have a photo of Rusty and you having your 'train time' because that is a routine you share together, right?" I asked.

"Right."

"And speaking of trains, Rusty is a child who would really enjoy a DVD series about emotions called 'The Transporters.' It is a series of videos using trains with human faces to teach emotions and an emotion vocabulary to children who, like your son, have a passion for trains but struggle to closely look at people's faces. I'll write down the link for you." I added it to the list.

"What a great idea! That sounds really interesting and perfect for Rusty!" Jennifer exclaimed.

"Yes, I agree. I think he will really enjoy it and increase his understanding and vocabulary about emotions. Plus I know you will enjoy sharing the learning time with him," I agreed.

There was one more area of strategies to discuss to complete the descriptive triangle.

"So before we stop for today, let's talk about visual ways to support Rusty in the area of sensory use and interests. Two key supports will help him become more flexible in making the transition from his preferred activities to following directions. The first one is creating transition routines whenever possible. Having him place objects into containers, like we did in here, visually signals the end of an activity for Rusty. The routine of putting things away is both organizing and regulating for him.

You can use bags, baskets, or any other form of containers. Pairing this with the visual 'first, then' card and his train schedule supports the behavior routine of increased flexibility when it comes to incoming demands. Does that make sense?"

Randy and Jennifer both agreed.

"The second key support is one you already are informally using with your son. And that it alternating work demands with sensory regrouping breaks. It would be helpful if you added the 'break' card as part of this routine. That way Rusty begins to make the association of 'break' with a short interval of time when he can anticipate that you will not be placing stressful incoming language or social demands on him. The repeated cycle of 'work/break/work/break' will help him anticipate the routine. Adding systematic, predictable sensory regrouping breaks will help Rusty develop more stamina in the area of not only tolerating incoming demands but also relaxing during nonpreferred activities and engaging in the learning process more completely. In other words, he'll spend less time trying to resist and avoid you and more time engaging with what you are trying to teach him or have him do."

"That makes so much sense," Jennifer said.

Randy added, "So what you're basically saying is if we start using the visual signals and add those to his routines Rusty will start to go with the flow more?"

"Exactly," I agreed.

Our time was almost up.

"We've talked about a lot of things today. So tell me, what are one or two main things you got out of this meeting?" I asked.

Jennifer went first. "Well, there was so much, but it really helped to see how much Rusty was able to do and how cooperative he was with the visual structure. And the train schedule and other visuals are going to be so helpful."

"For me, the most important thing was going through what it really means that my son has autism. That and showing us how important it is to take some pressure off of Rusty by making things more predictable. Thank you," Randy said with feeling.

"Thank you, It was such a pleasure meeting all of you and I am glad this was helpful."

"Let me make a copy of Rusty's Brain Style Profile and the recommended websites so you can take them with you. Then we can discuss setting up your next session."

Narrative Considerations with Young Children

Let's discuss the therapy process with Rusty and his parents. The parents had already received a diagnosis of autism for their son when they came in for their initial session. They were absorbing the emotional impact of the diagnosis and were looking for a way to better understand what it meant and what they needed to do to help their son. Beginning the session with sensory-based play with Rusty that centered on trains helped Rusty relax and show his range of strengths and differences. That led to the conversation with his parents about Rusty's individualized profile. Constructing Rusty's individualized profile laid the necessary groundwork to link practical supports to their emerging family story.

What specific narrative tools were used in this family session to support the shaping of their emerging family story?

- Starting the family session with sensory-based play provided Jennifer and Randy with an opportunity to watch their son engage in play in a new setting and interact with a new person in a cooperative way. This emphasized the importance of getting to know Rusty as a unique individual before starting a conversation about his diagnosis or recommended strategies. The story being told at the start of the session was the story of Rusty, not the story of autism.
- Inviting each parent to play with Rusty using the established format emphasized the emerging family story. Watching—and then applying—the routines created positive experiences for each parent. Their family story unfolded in this context as one of competence and expertise. Instead of emphasizing competence or expertise on the part of the clinician, they were able to experience their own power.
- Building Rusty's Brain Style Profile provided a document that underscored the family story of Rusty and his individuality. It gave his parents the necessary language to describe the world from their son's autism perspective with the emphasis on Rusty rather than on his diagnostic label. Listing key strategies and websites where they could research and learn more about the suggested visual supports supported the family narrative of competence and power.
- Organizing the discussion of visual supports into each of the three key areas (language and communication, social relationships and emotions, and sensory use and interests) anchored the suggested strategies into this family's individual narrative.
- Asking each parent to discuss the main points they were taking from the session provided another opportunity to develop their narrative. For Jennifer, the narrative as Rusty's mother was centered on using her understanding of her son's visual and systematic thinking style to set up visual routines. For Randy, having the language and framework to think about his son's brain style helped him process the emotional impact of Rusty's autism diagnosis in a way that fit with his day-to-day experiences with his son.

BOX 7.1 RUSTY'S BRAIN STYLE PROFILE

Language and Communication

Strengths

Ever increasing vocabulary for labeling;
Organizes, retrieves, and uses language best with visual contextual cues;
Using his language consistently to make requests;
Asks for help;
Learns and retains information well.

Differences

Low threshold for incoming language demands;
Language use primarily self-initiated and focused on labeling instead of
    social communication;
Not yet using shared social language;
Uses a somewhat scripted style of speech (exclamatory, loud).

Strategies

Visual schedule with pictures, words, and train track;
First/then card;
Websites with visual examples:
www.buildingblox.net
www.do2learn.com.

BOX 7.2 RUSTY'S BRAIN STYLE PROFILE

Social Relationships and Emotions

Strengths

Loving;
Enthusiastic;
Best laugh in the world;
Manages social stress by retreating into solitary play instead of becoming
    agitated or upset;
Starting to show shared enjoyment with preferred activities.

Differences

Difficulty noticing, responding to, and using simple social cues;
Responds best to exaggerated voice and facial expressions;

Withdraws from source of social demands;
Hard for him to participate in shared play;
Has not yet developed a labeling vocabulary to express his emotions.

Strategies

Interactive social photo books (me and my family; favorite places);
Website with train theme for teaching emotions:
www.thetransporters.com.

BOX 7.3 RUSTY'S BRAIN STYLE PROFILE

Sensory Use and Interests

Strengths

Strong memory for visual details;
Learns well with predictable visual routines;
Learns quickly and retains information well;
Self-regulates by engaging in self-directed activities with preferred
materials;
Visual thinker;
Systematic thinker.

Differences

Transition times can be difficult when he is engaged in a preferred activity;
Requires visual cues paired with verbal requests to successfully transition from one activity to the next.

Strategies

Transition routines (bags, containers);
Pair with "first/then" visual and train schedule;
Work/break/work/break routine.

Note

1   Brooks, Robert, and Goldstein, Sam (2012). *Raising Resilient Children with Autism Spectrum Disorders: Strategies for Helping Them Maximize Their Strengths, Cope with Adversity, and Develop a Social Mindset.* New York, NY: McGraw Hill.

8 Children

Identify the Main Therapeutic Conversation

- Each family brings a specific struggle into the therapeutic conversation.
- Autism-specific struggles during the childhood years often center on integrating the nature of the child's differences into the reality of family life projecting forwards.
- Themes include managing daily routines, coping with the impact of the child's inflexibility on the family system, and frustration with the child's school situation.

Link the Autism Narrative to the Experience of Mastery

- Help parents gain proficiency in taking the perspective of their child as a key component of the experience of mastery.
- Frame the parents as experts about their child.
- Emphasize the vitally important role their familiarity with their child plays in the development of creative and effective strategies.

Extend Supports beyond the Therapy Setting

- Understand the important role documents play in supporting families at this stage in the life cycle.
- Recognize the need for multiple sources of support for families.
- Become familiar with autism-specific community resources as well as reference materials for families.

Each family brings a unique and specific struggle into the therapeutic conversation. Autism specific struggles during the childhood years often center on integrating the nature of the child's differences into the reality of family life projecting forwards. The child's autism spectrum differences require daily support and energy from the parents. Parents help their child manage daily routines while coping with the stress the child's inflexibility places on the family system. As the child grows and matures, parents see the child's autism spectrum differences in increasingly sharper contrast to the development of typical peers. This contrast resonates within families as a reminder that autism is an incontrovertible part of the story, day after day and year after year. The differences may change their form and intensity but they are not going away. Plans must be made. The therapeutic conversation begins.

During the childhood years you can be most helpful to families when you link the autism narrative to the experience of mastery. Parents seek out clinicians who are knowledgeable about autism spectrum differences and perceive the clinician as a professional who possesses expertise. As part of this process they often overlook their role as experts about their specific child. Framing the parents as experts about their child is an important part of the narrative for families of children with autism spectrum differences. They are the people who are intimately familiar with the child. As you overtly emphasize the vitally important role of their expertise with their child you lay the groundwork for them to take ownership of the creative and effective strategies that will come out of your sessions together. The therapeutic conversation becomes a collaboration between clinician and parents. Parents experience a sense of their own expertise and mastery. The stress level in the family lessens as each family member experiences the power of the narrative of mastery.

Families raising a child with autism spectrum differences do best when they experience support from multiple sources. How supportive is the child's school team? Are extended family members understanding of the child with autism spectrum differences? How isolated or connected are the parents with other families who are part of the culture of autism? As a clinician, the more familiar you become with autism-specific community resources the more you can help parents experience mastery as they access the resources that are the best fit for them.

Documents play an important role in the therapeutic conversation at this stage in the family life cycle. Written lists that highlight the key points covered in the therapy session emphasize the development of capability, expertise, and proficiency for both parents and children.

What does the therapeutic conversation about mastery look like with families of children with autism spectrum differences? How are documents and resources introduced and discussed?

Oscar, His Parents, and the Therapeutic Conversation about Mastery

Oscar, his mother Joanna, and his father, Carson, had been working with me for several months. Oscar, a nine-year old with angular limbs that seem to project in multiple directions, had been working with his parents on gaining better control over his reactive, explosive behavior at home. His reactivity included yelling, stomping around the house, using threatening language while crowding into the personal space of others, and slamming doors. In our initial sessions I helped Oscar and his parents develop his autism Brain Style Profile. This document guided them in understanding the profound degree that Oscar's reactivity was related to his challenges in organizing and using his language and responding to incoming language demands. He also had tremendous difficulty shifting from his laser-focused agenda to the agenda of others. His chronic pattern of inflexibility created a high level of stress for this family.

Oscar had many areas of strength in addition to his daunting challenges. We had spent some time emphasizing his areas of competence while developing his autism Brain Style Profile. An additional document we had spent time creating in previous sessions was Oscar's self-regulation scale. His pattern was to alternate between his congenial, calm state to his reactive state or, in Oscar's words, "super mad and super frustrated." He participated in the development of his five-point regulation scale, including the identification of the words, actions, and feeling states that covered the range from calm to "super mad." He and his parents were encouraged to start a special notebook to store his brain style documents. Oscar brought it to each session, placing his documents inside for reference at home and at school.

The concept of "brain training" had been introduced and linked to Oscar's passionate interest in Pokemon. He was learning to train his brain in the same way he had to learn how to train his Pokemon to prepare for their epic and frequent battles. Oscar referred to the brain training process as "learning to control my powers."

Oscar and his parents were using the strategies at home and reported improvement in Oscar's ability to self-monitor and self-regulate. Let's join the session where Oscar was describing the shift he was experiencing since he began using his self-regulation scale.

Oscar sat with his feet perched on the edge of his chair, his knees level with his shoulders. He held a colorful plastic expanding sphere and opened and closed it as he organized his thoughts. His notebook was tucked under his chair.

"Okay, so my super mad, super frustrated ballistic self is still there. It used to be this massively big and bulky opponent and I had despair that I could never beat him." He quickly dropped his feet to the floor along with the expanding sphere and leaned forward. "But now he's like, this big." He placed his thumb and index finger several inches apart as he emphatically held up his right hand. "I know I can do this."

Joanna and Carson both smiled. His mother spoke first. "I like it that you are able to recognize when you are starting to go ballistic and that you're starting to gain control over your reactivity. We still have a ways to go but you are making a good start, Oscar."

Oscar listened attentively while gazing at a fixed point on the wall facing away from his parents.

His father added his comments. "I'm impressed with the way you described your explosive behavior, Oscar. That is a great way to think about it."

Oscar nodded once. "I still go ballistic sometimes."

"Like yesterday," Joanna said. She turned to me. "We need a plan for Oscar when he gets agitated so that he can calm down. He's getting agitated less often but it's still a big deal when he gets upset. We're definitely backing off and not talking to him as much when he gets agitated but he still traps us by following us around and ranting."

"So the routine is for Oscar to follow you around when he is at a level 4 or 5. Is that right, Oscar?" I asked.

"That's right."

"Is there a place in your house that you like to go to—a place that would be a good place to practice beating your opponent?"

Oscar didn't have to think very long to answer this question. "At school they have a special relaxation room that I go to for calming down. Or when I need a break. It has a bean bag and some pillows in it." He turned to his parents. "Hey, I know what would work. I need a special relax room at home. A double R." He turned to me. "Double R: relax room."

I wrote down: "Special relax room," "RR," and "Double R."

"So talk with your parents about setting up a double R space."

Oscar turned towards his parents. "Mom, don't we have a bean bag chair?"

"I think we do somewhere. If we can't find it you can come with me to pick one out." Joanna thought for a moment before continuing. "So would your relax spot be better in your room or downstairs? You could create a nook in your room pretty easily."

"You mean my Double R room. It will have to have a bean bag." Oscar was focused on the key details.

"Oscar, I am starting a list of what your Double R space is about. So we need to make a list of the important details. Are you ready to create your list?" I held up the notepad and Oscar looked at it and nodded in agreement.

"Put on there that I need a bean bag."

"Oscar, please take out your notebook and show me your self-regulation scale." I prompted him to reference the language we had already developed in a previous session. "Tell me what it says about your mind and body under number 1."

Oscar flung his notebook open and emphatically used his index finger as an arrow, landing on the wording on his scale under the number 1. "My mind and body are calm!"

"Yes, your mind and body are calm. So sometimes you need time to regroup at home and your mind and body have a better chance of becoming calm and organized if you know that you have a space where you can go that is only for that purpose: to get your mind and body calm and organized. Would you agree?"

"Yes, my Double R space. With a bean bag."

"So let's write a sentence that tells everyone what your Double R space is for. How about this sentence: 'When I am in my Double R space, that's the signal to leave me alone until my body and mind are calm and organized.'" I looked at Oscar, my pencil poised above the notepad.

"That's it!" Oscar nodded vigorously. He watched as I wrote the sentence.

"So Oscar, let's add a list of the objects you think would be helpful to have in your Double R space. Keep in mind that you will be using this space to train your brain to direct your body and mind to be calm and organized. It isn't a place where you will be playing electronic games. Can you tell me why I am suggesting that the Double R space be separate from playing electronic games?"

"Because when I play my games I get excited and I do not want to stop!" As he spoke he clenched his fists and shook his arms in front of his face. His face adopted an exaggerated grimace and his voice volume notably rose.

"Exactly. And that gets in the way of training your brain to regroup. So what would help you have a calm mind and body?"

"Music." He snapped his head in the direction of his parents. "I could listen to the CDs I have liked all of my life. Baby Mozart! Lullaby Classics!" He named his preferred music.

His father nodded. "Headphones would be a good idea, don't you think?"

"Great idea, Dad! Headphones it is!" Oscar turned to me. "Write that down, please."

I wrote: "bean bag," "quiet music (Baby Mozart, Lullaby Classics)," and "headphones" while Oscar supervised. "This is a good plan, Oscar. Can you think of anything else you would like to add to this list?"

"Pillows. I like to squeeze pillows while I listen to music with my headphones."

"Great. I'll add pillows to the list."

There was another aspect to this plan that needed to be addressed. I directed Oscar back to his regulation scale. "So Oscar, as you look at your scale, what level would be the best level for you to practice training your brain to use the Double R space? Should you wait until you are at level 5?"

"That would be too late. I think I should use it at level 4."

"Good thinking," his father said.

His mother added her thoughts. "Maybe you could even use it some-times when you are at level 3. Sometimes a break from everything while you're still calm might help you not go ballistic later."

"Great idea, Mom!"

"Thanks. Would it help if we reminded you sometimes or asked you if you wanted to use your Double R space?"

Oscar nodded. "You and Dad could do that."

I wrote "Use my Double R space when I am at level 3 or level 4" on the list. I handed the list to Oscar and asked him to read it aloud. He did.

I addressed the three of them with another idea. "This Double R plan is a good one to help Oscar practice training his brain to get his mind and body to stay calm and organized. But I think we need to talk about a plan, or a routine, to set up for Oscar to use when he has a lot of energy and needs to move around and work some of that energy off." I turned to Oscar.

"What do you think, Oscar? When your body is full of energy you might need to have a way to work it out. Going to a quiet area might not be the best fit at those times."

He nodded. "Like when I am in my Pokemon mode and I have the combined energy of Grass, Fire, Water, Lightning and Psychic energy cards!" He hopped up and assumed a battle stance.

"Exactly. Lots of energy. But positive energy, right?"

"Positive energy!" He repeated his stance.

"So on your scale, where are you when you have lots of energy, Oscar?" I asked.

"It depends. When I am full of Pokemon energy, that is, happy energy, I am at level 1." He contorted his face into a deep scowl. "But when I am full of frustration I am at a level 5!"

His mother agreed with Oscar. "And when you are at a level 5 you fol-low us around and rant and yell and won't back down."

"So we need a plan or routine for you to systematically manage your energy needs, Oscar," I said. I held up my notepad. "How about a move-ment plan?"

"Okay." Oscar stood in front of me expectantly.

I turned towards Joanna and Carson. "What are your thoughts about a movement plan?"

Carson thought for a moment. "Oscar does a lot of pacing at times. Sometimes when I see him pacing I ask him to take the dog for a walk. That way they both work off some energy."

"Great idea, Dad!" he turned to me. "Write down 'walk around the block with Maisie' please."

I wrote down: "Walk around the block with Maisie until my body and mind are calm and organized." I held it out to Oscar so he could read it.

Carson had some additional thoughts on this topic. "I've been talking for a while now about hanging up a punching bag in the garage for Oscar. I was thinking it would be a good way for him to work off some of his excess energy when he starts to get wound up." He turned to Oscar.

"What do you think about going with me to pick out a bag and you can help me hang it up and use it as one of your brain training tools?"

"Great idea, Dad!" Oscar jumped up and down, shaking his fists in the air, before walking over to his father and giving him a brisk hug. In the middle of the hug he whipped his head around and directed me to add the punching bag to the list.

"So we have two new plans for you to practice at home, Oscar. Read this second plan aloud." I handed him the list and he read it in a serious voice with the paper held out at arm's length. He ended his recitation by flapping the paper several times before placing it in his notebook and slamming it shut.

"Great work in here today, Oscar!" I said. "Tell me what you're remembering from our work today."

"Double R! Walk with Maisie! Punching bag shopping with Dad! Train the brain and beat the opponent!" He marched in small circles while reciting the events from the session. He stopped in his tracks in front of his mother. Oscar leaned over and hugged her. "Your turn, Mom. What do you remember from our work here today?"

His mother struggled to contain her laughter and assumed a serious expression. "That you are amazing. And I'll help you set up the Double R space."

Carson looked at his family with unmistakable affection. He turned towards me. "You know, when Oscar was first diagnosed we took it on as if we were starting a sprint. But as he's gotten older and his world has become more complex I've come to think of this process as more of a long distance run. And today we worked on another milestone or marker on the route."

"Beautifully put, Carson. You and your family are definitely forging your own path. Today your insight into your son's need for physical movement led to the development of a plan to help him add to his brain training tool kit. I look forward to hearing about how the punching bag and Double R action plans turn out."

The Therapy Process with Oscar and His Parents

Let's discuss the therapy process with Oscar and his parents. The therapeutic conversation in the initial sessions introduced the experience of mastery through the construction of two essential documents.

• First, Oscar and his parents individualized their understanding of Oscar's autism diagnosis through the construction of his Brain Style Profile. This process helped the family focus on Oscar's areas of strength and competency. The narrative expanded to include his capabilities, placing the stressful episodes of his explosive behavior into a context of hopefulness instead of despair. As each family member contributed to the narrative, a sense of collaboration emerged.

They were in this together, and "this" was shifting from the experience of a never-ending cycle of stressful episodes to the experience of finding creative ways for Oscar to "train his brain."

- The second essential document created in the early sessions was Oscar's self-regulation scale. The creation of the scale served several purposes. It externalized his reactivity as something that could be identified as words and actions. Where Oscar's reactivity was initially experienced as binary (*"super happy"* or *"super frustrated"*) the scale allowed for a visual representation of the range of states of being. The words, actions, and feelings states were named and filled in on Oscar's scale, including the midpoints. This externalization of his reactive behavior provided Oscar and his parents with a way to talk about his need to self-monitor and self-regulate in a neutral, matter-of-fact way. It was a key document in their process of collaboration to, in Oscar's words, *"beat the opponent."*

- Encouraging Oscar and his parents to create a notebook to store his documents further defined the process as of one of mastery. Oscar had a concrete, externalized system that he was adding to during each of the family sessions. The family had a physical point of reference for the tools they were putting into place to support Oscar's self-monitoring and self-regulation skills. Having the notebook available during the session allowed for the experience of having Oscar reference the language developed in previous sessions as new documents and strategies were developed during subsequent sessions. (*"Oscar, please take out your notebook and show me your self-regulation scale . . . tell me what it says about your mind and body under number 1."*).

Following the development of the two essential documents and the resulting experience of mastery, the subsequent sessions focused on supporting the progress the family was experiencing as they implemented the strategies at home.

- Introducing the link between Oscar's passionate interest in Pokemon and his goal-directed task of "training his brain" helped Oscar create a powerful metaphor. He was able to externalize his reactivity and perceive it as an opponent with which he had to do battle. Asking him to discuss how the process of using his self-regulation scale was going for him led to Oscar's depiction of how he was gaining mastery over his *"super frustrated ballistic self."* He described going from a state of powerlessness (*"I had despair that I could never beat him."*) to a sense of competence and mastery (*"But now he's like, this big . . . I know I can do this."*).

- Establishing a place for Oscar to use as his consistent regrouping location in the house (his *"Double R space"*) built on the foundation laid with his self-regulation scale. Creating the document during the session gave his family a goal-directed plan to follow. Placing Oscar in charge of reading the plan and storing it in his notebook reinforced the process of his acquisition of mastery and control over his reactive behavior.

- While serving as the documentarian I was able to encourage Oscar and his parents to craft the details of Oscar's "*Double R space*" plan. Each family member added valuable suggestions and details to individualize the plan to develop Oscar's regrouping space at home. During this session Oscar and his parents practiced having a conversation that emphasized their competencies and their ability to collaborate, strengthening the family system. Oscar, Joanna, and Carson were the experts in crafting the plan.
- Since Oscar was continuing to pursue his parents at home when he was in a highly agitated state, I brought up the need for a self-regulation routine that involved physical movement. Once the concept was introduced the family was able to discuss ways to set up a goal-directed plan. Documenting this plan added to their set of mastery tools.
- The mood and tone of the family shifted from stress and defeat to collaboration and affection. Ending the session with a prompt to review the main things each family member was taking from the meeting provided an opportunity to highlight these feelings of competence and well-being. Oscar practiced his sense of mastery by reciting the list of goal-directed tasks discussed during the session. Joanna expressed her affection for her son and her willingness to collaborate with him in setting up his special space. Carson used a powerful metaphor to reflect on the process that was taking place since Oscar received his diagnosis.

Marcus and Anna Seek Out Support in Relation to Emma's School Program

During the initial sessions with Marcus, his wife Anna, and their seven-year-old-daughter Emma, the main therapeutic conversation centered on the theme of improving Emma's school situation. Although Emma had a diagnosis of Autism Spectrum Disorder, her school did not recognize the diagnosis. Instead, they told her parents that Emma was a child who displayed emotional and behavioral problems. They acknowledged that Emma displayed some characteristics of autism, especially as reported by her parents, but interpreted her behaviors in school as willful and purposeful. They noted that because Emma made eye contact with others and had an active imagination, autism was not the best way to describe her differences. They developed a behavior plan that consisted of verbal prompts and consequences for her behavior. Emma was receiving some special education support in the form of an assistant in her first-grade classroom. The assistant was there to provide the verbal prompts and to escort Emma out of the classroom when she became too disruptive. When she had to be removed from the classroom she was taken to the office where she sat with the assistant in the principal's office or the counselor's office until she was ready to return to the classroom. On several occasions when Emma had refused to leave the classroom the teacher took the entire class out of the room until Emma calmed down and could be removed.

The first goal with this family was to get to know Emma and her worldview. This was accomplished through several play-based sensory sessions with Emma and her parents. Emma's diagnosis of autism spectrum differences was confirmed and her Brain Style Profile was completed. In the first sessions, strategies and supports for use with Emma at home were discussed. As her parents implemented the suggested strategies they reported a positive shift in Emma's behavior at home. School behavior remained the focus of unresolved concern.

The session we will be joining was with Marcus and Anna and was focused on discussing her school needs. Emma was not included in this session.

"We really want her school team to understand what makes Emma tick. At home, we know that she needs her down time to play with her stuffed animals and draw her pictures. We know that she needs to know what's coming next and that she does well with our lists and schedules. And since we've been coming here we've seen a lot of improvement in her ability to handle demands since we started using the visual supports more consistently." Marcus was the spokesperson for his family and he began the session by emphasizing the goal of helping Emma's school understand her through the lens of her autism spectrum differences.

Marcus continued.

"After our last meeting we set up a conference at her school and we shared Emma's profile with them. They were receptive to the language and agreed that the profile described the child they see at school. They really do want to help her but they don't seem to know what to do beyond what they're doing now."

Anna added her observations.

"They definitely have good intentions, but honestly, they don't seem to know what to do to support Emma. There was some progress in the last meeting when they agreed on how we see Emma through her Brain Style Profile. So now we need some specific recommendations on what they can add to her school program. Having an adult attached to her is not enough. She's starting to tell us that she doesn't want to go to school."

Because the Brain Style Profile had been positively reviewed by Emma's school team, I brought up the suggestion that an additional document detailing recommended strategies would also be helpful in moving Emma's school program forward.

"That's great that the school team are now in agreement with you about how Emma sees the world. But it sounds like they are still struggling to develop effective strategies and supports for her. So let's talk about what strategies will be most helpful for Emma at school and organize our conversation around her style. Would that be helpful?"

Marcus and Anna agreed.

"As we discussed in our last session, behavior is communication. So we have to organize the suggestions for Emma's school plan in a way that addresses what Emma's school behavior is communicating." I paused before continuing.

"Based on her brain style and also on the positive changes you've seen at home as you've started to consistently use some of the visual supports we've discussed in here, Emma's behavior is communicating: too much! Too many demands, too many transitions, too much language, and too much social input. And when Emma begins to communicate: too much! What happens to her behavior?"

"That's when she refuses to do things and then it escalates into all of the yelling, falling on the floor, and crying," Anna said.

"And now we understand that she has created these routines to deal with the stress of incoming demands," Marcus added. "As we communicated this to the school staff they were able to accept that this is the case as well. That's the first step to getting a positive plan in place."

"Exactly. So let's discuss the positive plan and then I'll write a summary you can use as your talking points when you work with her school team to develop the plan."

As I described the three key areas and strategies for Emma I wrote the key points, creating a document for the Anna and Marcus.

"Emma's autism spectrum differences clearly affect her ability to manage in school in three main areas: organization, regulation, and social understanding." I wrote each of the three key terms on the page.

"Let's start with organization. Emma needs to have a consistent way to predict and anticipate her school routine. Even though she knows the basic routine, a visual schedule would help her organize her behavior." I wrote this down and continued. "Think about how adding her visual schedule has helped at home."

Marcus and Anna both nodded. "It's really helped her gain a sense of control over her day. She loves checking things off of her list. And she is less anxious than she used to be," Anna observed.

Marcus added his thoughts. "The mini-schedules are also helpful—the 'first/then' chart and the chart where we show her what she is working for. All have made a difference."

"So visual supports—a daily schedule, first/then charts, charts that show how much work and what comes next—those are things we'll add under the general category of organization. Keeping those schedules and visual tools in an organizational notebook, and having an adult coach her on the use of the visual supports will be helpful for Emma." I wrote those items on the list.

I continued. "And of course, a reminder to talk less and to show while telling is important for Emma." I added those to the list. "In the school setting, job cards, or cards that list out the steps involved in a task, are additional visual organizational tools she would respond well to. It gives the adults a way to direct her to her list instead of having to verbally cue her for each step. It gives Emma a step-by-step visual map to follow."

"When Emma was in here with me, I noticed that she organized her behavior best when she was able to manipulate objects and put them into categories and produce some sort of order. And you described her play at home as systematic with her stuffed animals, books, and drawings."

"That's right," her mother and father agreed.

"So using manipulative materials when teaching her will probably be very helpful. Using folder tasks, for example, where her work is in a folder and she has to organize the materials according to the concept being taught." I added this to the list.

"What are your thoughts about these suggestions?" I asked.

Marcus took a moment to review the list while Anna did the same.

"I think this is quite helpful. It gives us a way to have a dialogue with her school team so we can be specific in telling them what goals we would like to have in place for her in the classroom." Marcus spoke for both of them while Anna nodded in agreement.

"Yes, I think this will be helpful," I agreed. "Let's move on to the area of supports for Emma in the area of regulation. At home, you are already using her self-regulation scale, and developing one at school will be helpful for her in that setting." I added this suggestion to the list in the regulation section.

"Just as she does at home, Emma would benefit from systematic sensory regrouping breaks throughout the day. Managing all of the incoming language, social, work, and sensory demands at school is hard work for Emma. Breaking her day into more manageable blocks of time will reduce her reactivity to demands. Deciding where in the classroom and where in the school building Emma can take her sensory regrouping breaks will be important details to discuss."

Marcus and Anna nodded in agreement and I continued.

"We've talked about the two of you using the idea of training her brain at home, along with identifying her 'words and actions' that she is learning to use to replace her yelling, refusing, and crying behavior routines. Let's add that to the school recommendations list."

Marcus added an observation. "We'll have to talk with the school about having someone teach her to use the tools after they have been developed."

"That's right. As you set up her specific goals part of your plan will include discussing who will be responsible for developing the materials and teaching the skills to Emma."

Anna added her thoughts. "Between the special education teacher, the school counselor, and the visiting school psychologist they should be able to develop this plan for Emma." Marcus nodded in agreement.

"So that brings us to the third area of supports for Emma: social understanding," I said. "You've already shared Emma's Brain Style Profile with her school team. So if they can help her develop a school notebook about herself that can be completed over time, with Emma gathering facts and information about not only herself but also her classmates, that would be really helpful for her in the area of increasing her social narrative and social understanding."

I added those suggestions to her list.

Marcus added his suggestion. "They really need to teach her social skills directly because she isn't going to pick them up in a natural way. So we should add that to the list."

"Exactly," I agreed, as I added his social skills recommendation to the list.

"Is there anything else you can think of that you would like to add to this list?" I asked. "Do you think this gives you a good foundation to move the conversation forward?"

Marcus and Anna looked at each other as they thought about the items on the list. Marcus spoke first.

"No, no, this is very helpful. If you could put it into a formal document for us then we will add it to her Brain Style Profile and discuss the recommendations with her school team."

"Of course. I would be happy to."

Anna added her thoughts after lightly resting her fingertips on her husband's sleeve.

"This is most helpful; I agree. But there is only so much the school can do. Can you recommend any place where we could take Emma to join a social group to work on her social skills development? Don't you agree, Marcus?"

Marcus nodded in agreement. "Yes, yes, any suggestions are welcome."

"There are several excellent people who provide social skills groups for school-aged children. I'll give you their contact information. I'd also suggest that you look into going to one of the local parent support groups for children with autism spectrum differences. You'll meet other parents who will be able to tell you their experiences and recommendations about social skills groups and other resources. The group I recommend has monthly social gatherings organized by age groups for children while the parents meet."

BOX 8.1 EMMA'S SCHOOL DOCUMENT

Emma would benefit from specific, systematic interventions to help her in the areas of *organization* and *regulation* of her behavior. Emma would also benefit from the development of her *self-determination narrative*.

- In the area of *organization*, Emma would benefit from the following:
  ○ Visual schedule;
  ○ Talk less, and show while telling using visual supports (schedule, "first/then" card, job cards, T-chart for words and actions);
  ○ Organizational notebook with systematic adult coaching to master routine of using it throughout the day;
  ○ Work organized with visual step-by-step maps;
  ○ Increased use of manipulative materials when teaching concepts.
- In the area of *regulation*, Emma would benefit from the following:
  ○ Self-regulation scale and prompts throughout the day to rate: "How am I doing?";
  ○ Systematic sensory regrouping breaks planned into her day in a proactive way;
  ○ "Words and actions" T-chart to identify and build adaptive replacement behavior routines;
  ○ Introduce the concept of "train my brain" to teach adaptive coping skills routines.
- In the area of *social understanding*, Emma would benefit from the following:
  ○ Develop a notebook about Emma that contains all of her tools;
  ○ Include her personal narrative in the notebook, built with her over time, with her Brain Style Profile; narrative about herself and her life; and her skills, talents, and goals;
  ○ Direct teaching of social skills with opportunities to practice skills with her same-age peers.

The Therapy Process with Marcus and Anna

The therapy process for Marcus and Anna focused on the main therapeutic conversation of finding effective ways to communicate their concerns to Emma's school team. They were not adversarial in their relationship with the school but were clearly in disagreement with the way the school staff were perceiving their daughter and managing her needs. They had direct experience with the benefit of the visual support strategies, as they had successfully incorporated the supports into their home life.

The session focused on the development of a document that would give them the language and organization of suggested strategies to promote a positive conversation with Emma's school team. The document focused on three main areas.

- The area of organization was discussed, with specific suggestions listed under that heading. This was followed by a discussion of regulation strategies. Strategies to support Emma's social understanding rounded out the list.
- The development of a final document was recommended, as this gave the parents the support they needed to align themselves as experts on what their daughter needed in a school program. They could approach the school meeting as a conversation in which they were informed and knowledgeable about their daughter and her specific needs, emphasizing their role as experts who have developed specific competencies in supporting their daughter's development.
- Emma's mother brought up the fact that the school could not meet all of Emma's needs. She requested additional outside resources. Recommending practitioners who provide social skills groups and training, and parent support groups that also provide opportunities for children with autism spectrum differences to have social experiences, added to this family's sense of mastery. It helped them move their positive narrative forward.

9 Adolescents

Key Autism Differences that Interfere with Adaptive Adolescent Development

- Autism differences create a distinctively lower threshold for the simultaneous management of language, social, and sensory information.
- Executive functioning skills are often less developed than those of same-age peers, resulting in conflict between ongoing dependency of adults to support these functions and the drive for autonomy.
- Being out of sync with peers often results in a negative self-narrative.

Key Narrative Therapy Themes for Adolescents with Autism Spectrum Differences

- Development of a positive conceptualization of self.
- Recognition and management of emotions.
- Transition from prompt-dependency to autonomy.

Key Narrative Therapy Components to Shape the Understanding of Autism Spectrum Differences for the Adolescent and His or Her Family

- Use of descriptive language to shape the understanding of the adolescent's distinctive style or worldview.
- Reframe deficits as differences.
- Link the understanding of differences to skills that support autonomy and emotional resiliency.

Depression, anxiety, and behavioral outbursts often lead parents to seek out therapy for their children during the adolescent years. A growing number of adolescents seen by clinicians have a long-standing diagnosis of Autism Spectrum Disorder, and their families are driven to seek out therapy when the adolescent overtly shows signs of increased stress, agitation, and depression. It is not uncommon for adolescents with autism spectrum differences to experience feelings of despair when they struggle with recognizing that they are different from their peers. Many young people express the observation "my brain doesn't work right" as they struggle to make sense out of why the social world is so challenging for them. When social failure is experienced, and when regulation of emotions during interactions with others is unattainable, the logical conclusion reached by many adolescents with autism spectrum differences becomes: "I want to die," or "I want to kill myself."[1]

Imagine how exponentially more distressing it is for adolescents and their parents when the adolescent has not yet been given a diagnosis of autism spectrum differences. When there is no context to understand the underlying reasons contributing to the adolescent's out of sync behaviors and feelings in relation to his or her peers, the stress experienced by the family can be quite high. This is frequently the case for female adolescents with underlying autism spectrum differences, as they are often identified as experiencing depression and anxiety. In treating the symptoms of depression and anxiety, the underlying autism differences are frequently overlooked by clinicians.[2]

Without an understanding of autism spectrum brain style differences, the adolescent narrative often centers on emotional coping deficits. Areas of strength and ability are often lost in the wake of this powerful negative narrative.

What are some of the key autism spectrum differences that interfere with adaptive adolescent development?

Autism spectrum differences create a distinctively lower threshold for the simultaneous management of language, social, and sensory information. The daily routine of school places demands on the adolescent that oftentimes require engagement with language, social, and high-stimulation settings that surpass the individual's coping threshold. Adolescents with autism spectrum differences require additional time to focus on their preferred interests and rely on retreating into routines involving their preferred interests as a means of regulating and managing the demands of their increasingly complex and stressful social world.

Even for highly verbal adolescents with autism spectrum differences, processing incoming language can be stressful and requires a great deal of concentrated energy. The adolescent with autism spectrum differences experiences incoming language as somewhat unpredictable, in that the adolescent is unable to place incoming language into a social context. When language is paired with social communication demands, as it almost always is in communication between peers, the adolescent with spectrum differences experiences significantly greater stress. This leads to emotional regulation challenges, which leads to a shut down in the individual's ability to process, organize, retrieve, and use language in a fluid and reciprocal way. In contrast, when the adolescent with autism spectrum differences initiates conversation on his or her preferred topic, more complex language is used, albeit in a one-sided way. This contrast in the ability to apply language skills is important for the clinician to understand, as the adolescent may require extra time to process information during therapeutic conversations and may not have the necessary vocabulary to express emotions and to describe internal states without direct teaching during therapy sessions.

For adolescents with autism spectrum differences, executive functioning skills are often less developed than those of their same-age peers. All adolescents are in the process of developing executive functioning skills; that is, the ability to control and coordinate thoughts and behavior. Compared to typically developing adolescents, those with autism spectrum differences struggle in their decision-making abilities, working memory, initiation, inhibition, emotional regulation abilities, and organizational skills. These skill deficits are often in conflict with the adolescent's drive for increased autonomy from parental supervision and control. When the clinician helps the adolescent and his or her parents develop an understanding of the individual's executive functioning challenges, and places this understanding in the context of autism spectrum brain differences, it becomes possible to develop a plan to teach the key skills that will lead to autonomy in daily life.

Managing peer relationships becomes a major source of stress and anxiety for the adolescent with autism spectrum differences. The adolescent with differences is caught between a desire for successful peer relationships and connections and a growing awareness of being out of sync with his or her peers. This often translates into a negative self-narrative, with the adolescent with spectrum differences perceiving him or herself as defective or diminished in capacity. The individual may retreat into solitary exploration of his or her areas of preferred interest, may avoid school and social gatherings, and may interact with others only through online contact. This opting out of adolescent social experiences can lead to social isolation and limit college and employment options as the adolescent makes the transition to young adult life.

The narrative therapy themes for clinicians working with adolescents on the autism spectrum focus on shaping the use of descriptive language. Descriptive language is used to shape the understanding of the adolescent's distinctive brain style or worldview. Deficits are reframed as differences, opening the door to the development of effective coping tools and strategies. Once deficits are conceptualized as differences, it becomes possible to link the understanding of differences to skills that support autonomy and emotional resiliency. Developing the adolescent's Brain Style Profile emphasizes a narrative that focuses on positive qualities. An integral part of this process is shaping the recognition and management of emotions.

The shaping of a positive self-narrative provides a platform to support the adolescent's transition from prompt-dependency on adults to self-initiation and autonomy. To a greater degree than is the case for neuro-typical adolescents, individuals with autism spectrum differences rely on adults to manage daily tasks. Organization, planning, regulation of emotions, and inhibiting impulses are common areas of executive functioning challenges that place the adolescent with autism spectrum differences in the position of relying on trusted adults to anticipate areas of need and make necessary accommodations. As the adolescent works with a skilled clinician to develop a self-narrative that includes an understanding of the types of supports he or she is receiving from parents and teachers, it becomes possible to develop age-appropriate autonomy.

What would the application of these concepts and themes look like in a therapy session with an adolescent with autism spectrum differences? Amelia's initial session provides an example of how to approach these key elements when the adolescent has not yet been given a formal diagnosis of Autism Spectrum Disorder.

Amelia and Her Parents Start the Conversation about Her Brain Style Differences

Amelia, a 16-year-old high school student, struggled for years with anxiety and depression. I met Amelia and her parents when they contacted me after their last counselor brought up the possibility that Amelia might have a high-functioning form of autism spectrum disorder and gave the family my name.

Her parents first sought out help for their daughter when she was six years old. The staff at her school told them that Amelia was a creative, bright child who was shy. In school, Amelia kept to herself, maintained good grades, and was not identified as having any particular issues or needs. As she moved through her school years, however, Amelia struggled in several areas. She tended to isolate herself during social times like lunch, recess, and breaks, and did not establish any genuine friendships with her peers. When she interacted with her classmates it was almost always to correct them or to tell them what to do. She preferred the company of her teachers. Amelia became visibly nervous when she was in large group settings and on more than one occasion during a fire drill she was found cowering in a corner of the classroom while the alarm went off.

At home, a complex story was unfolding. Before school in the mornings Amelia cried and panicked on a daily basis. Although she was able to pull herself together and make it through each school day, the effort took a toll on her energy level and sense of well-being. She needed large amounts of time at home to be by herself and became irritable and upset when simple demands were made of her. Her parents sought help for Amelia with a psychiatrist. They were told after the initial visit that Amelia was anxious and depressed and needed medication, which was prescribed. Therapy was also recommended. Her parents found a psychologist and started taking Amelia to regular appointments.

The psychologist also told Amelia's parents that their daughter was struggling with anxiety and depression. During the ongoing sessions with the psychologist, Amelia routinely sat in a slumped posture and was minimally responsive to the questions posed by her counselor. This lack of participation in the therapy conversation served to confirm the therapist's belief that Amelia was a child who was anxious and depressed. Amelia went through a cycle of changing medications and therapists that continued into her early adolescent years. The words "depression" and "anxiety" became an integral part of her identity and of the family's story.

But what exactly was behind this seemingly lifelong depression and anxiety? Her parents experienced living with a daughter who had two distinctly different sides to her. When Amelia was not in school, she preferred to stay at home with her parents. Her favorite activities were drawing and watching YouTube videos of animals. From the time she was a young girl she had been an enthusiastic fan of the cartoon series "My Little Pony," a passion that continued into her adolescence. Her creative drawings often incorporated features of the characters from this cartoon program.

At home, Amelia displayed a strong drive to spend time by herself and appeared relaxed and happy when she was able to do so. Unexpected changes in routine were a source of stress and agitation for her and she did best with advanced notice. Amelia had a strong set of particular interests and activities she preferred at home and she became agitated and upset when those routines were interrupted. Since starting in her high school program she had met several peers who shared some of her interests and with whom she felt comfortable. For the first time in her life Amelia seemed to be forming genuine friendships but she declined most invitations to meet her friends for activities outside of school.

When I first met Amelia and her parents, Patricia and Trevor, all three of them appeared downcast. Here they were meeting with yet another psychologist. Each of them took a seat: slump-shouldered, reserved, quiet. I took a moment to gather my thoughts before starting our conversation. I looked at Amelia as she sat next to her parents, her eyes on a framed picture showing colorful paper cut-outs of a school of fish. She studied the details closely. I noticed Amelia was wearing brightly colored socks with ponies on them.

"The artist that made that makes her own paper before creating her designs," I said, referring to the picture.

Amelia and her parents silently looked at the artwork.

"Do you know what she calls this particular piece?"

In unison they shook their heads.

"Right fish, wrong school."

Amelia jutted her head closer to the picture.

"Huh," she said and nodded her head. "One of the fish has a unique feature."

"Exactly. By the way I really like your socks."

She stuck her feet out and twirled her ankles, gazing at her socks, acknowledging my compliment. After a pause she made a declaration.

"I never wear matching ones. This is Rainbow Dash." Amelia stuck out her left foot. "And this is Fluttershy."

"Very cool. My Little Pony has been around for quite some time, hasn't it?"

I noticed that Amelia took a few extra minutes before she responded; a little longer than most people. "Hasbro created the original My Little Pony in 1983. They were called the Rainbow Ponies and are now highly prized collector's items. The latest series is 'My Little Pony: Friendship Is Magic.' I've collected most of the ponies in the current series." Amelia's demeanor changed dramatically as she began sharing information about one of her areas of passionate interest with me. She sat up and radiated energy. She made fleeting eye contact with me. Her voice volume increased and she spoke with a distinctive cadence, enunciating each word clearly, with a slight nasal intonation.

"What do you like the most about 'My Little Pony: Friendship Is Magic?'" I asked, matching my speaking style to hers.

Amelia's eyebrows knit together as she thought about this. "Well, actually I like everything about the show. Even though it may be for little kids I still like it. As you may be able to tell by the name of the show it is about friendship and other important lessons. I guess I would say I like the lessons it teaches me. And of course I love the ponies!"

Patricia and Trevor followed our conversation closely. They also appeared more alert and engaged, as they watched their daughter enthusiastically share information instead of slumping in her chair as they had seen her do so many times in the past.

"Tell me more about Rainbow Dash—isn't that this one?" I asked as I pointed to the character on her left foot.

Amelia went on to share detailed information about her beloved program and the characters and their qualities. She was relaxed and comfortable, as were her parents. It was time to ask about the story of anxiety and depression that they brought with them.

"Amelia, you seem quite relaxed and happy as you share information with me about 'My Little Pony: Friendship Is Magic.' Are there other activities you do or settings when you feel this way?"

"Well, I also like to draw and create characters. And I like to watch cats do crazy things on YouTube." She looked over at her mother. "And I like to bake pies sometimes with my mom. And Dad likes it when we make rhubarb pie."

"So you like spending time at home?"

"I would like it if I could stay home all of the time."

I turned to Amelia's parents. "What do you think about this? Does Amelia seem relaxed and happy at home sometimes?"

Patricia nodded. "As long as Amelia has time to spend by herself things go well. It's when she has to get out in the world that things get difficult."

"Would you agree, Amelia?" I asked.

"Yes, like I said: I would like it if I could stay home all the time." She repeated her previous observation, saying it in the exact same way. It sounded like this was a sentence she said to herself often.

"School has always been a trigger for stress," Patricia continued. "Even with the medication Amelia cries every morning before she gets out of the car and goes into the building."

"Tell me more about that, Amelia."

Amelia's face contorted into a grimace and her whole body visibly tensed. She began tapping her right fist on her thigh. "I don't know." She paused between each word, emphasizing each with a thump.

Trevor spoke up. "This is how it starts."

I addressed Amelia directly. "It sounds like it takes a lot of energy to get ready to face the school day."

Both her parents started talking at once. Amelia's tapping on her thigh turned into pounding.

"I'm telling you, this has been going on since first grade . . . We're almost at the point to just do home schooling but that wouldn't really solve anything."

"We've tried everything; nothing seems to make a difference. She just can't seem to tolerate discussing this topic. She just wants us to leave her alone."

They turned their focus from explaining things to me and directed their comments to their daughter.

"Come on Amelia; just talk about it. What bothers you so much about school? You seem to be able to manage pretty well once you're there. Just tell us. You've told us before that the noise and commotion bother you. Is it the noise? The people? The other kids?"

Amelia's agitation level increased in intensity the longer her parents talked. In addition to pounding on her leg she kept repeating the phrase "I don't know!" Her voice became louder with each repetition, effectively drowning out the comments made by her parents.

I stretched my arms out in front of me, with the palms of my hands facing out.

"Stop talking," I said firmly and distinctly.

"But Amelia . . . ," Patricia started.

"You need to know . . . ," Trevor blurted out.

"I don't know!" Amelia shouted.

"STOP TALKING."

Everyone stopped talking. Amelia's pounding ceased almost immediately. We sat in silence for a minute but I'm fairly certain it seemed like much longer to her parents. After about 30 seconds we watched the tension release itself from Amelia's body.

"Better?" I asked.

"Better," Amelia replied.

"Can you listen while I talk to your parents?"

After a beat Amelia answered, "Yes."

I turned to Patricia and Trevor. "So what just happened is typical, yes?"

Taking their cue from me they kept their answers brief. "Yes. We're glad you saw that. That's what we see at home all the time."

"So when Amelia is talking about her beloved ponies *she* is picking the topic and *you* are listening." I paused here to give Amelia time to absorb what I was saying without becoming overwhelmed by too much verbal input.

I directed my next comment to Amelia. "So Amelia, I noticed that when I asked you questions about 'My Little Pony' you thought carefully before you gave me an answer." I paused for a moment. "So you are someone who is a careful thinker. You take your time before you answer."

Amelia was listening to this intently. She nodded.

"So I'm guessing when other people, like your parents, start asking you questions sometimes there is not enough time to think about your answer before they ask another question."

Another pause. Another nod.

"And that is especially true when they ask you about your feelings and school. Yes?"

Another nod. "And also when they ask me a lot of questions and I'm trying to concentrate on my stuff at home," Amelia added.

"So it isn't only questions about school that upset you."

Amelia shook her head. "Too many questions."

"It looks like when your parents ask you questions you go from the *thinking* part of your brain to the *reacting* part . . ."

". . . and it makes it really hard to talk or to listen to others talk."

Amelia nodded.

"Can you tell me what you say and do when the talking and the feelings get to be too much?"

Amelia thought about this. "I pound my leg. I say 'I don't know.'"

I nodded. "Yes, that's what you just did. You pounded your leg and you said 'I don't know' many times."

I turned back to Patricia and Trevor.

"And when Amelia says 'I don't know' you try to help her figure that out by talking to her and asking her questions, right?"

Both her parents nodded. "We're just trying to help her figure this out."

"Of course," I said. I turned to Amelia. "You know they're just trying to help you, right?"

"But it's not helping." She pounded her thigh for emphasis.

"Let's see if we can come up with a way to help them help you."

I continued. "When you tell them 'I don't know' is it possible that what you are really trying to tell them is 'Stop talking?'"

Amelia thought about this. "Well, I am polite so what I really mean is 'Please stop talking.'"

I turned to her parents. "When Amelia is upset and you want to help her, and she says 'I don't know,' of course you try to help her by trying to figure out what it is she doesn't know. As you try to figure it out you ask her questions. Is that about right?"

Trevor spoke up for both of them. "That's pretty much how it happens. We start with the 20 questions: 'Is it this? Is it that?'"

"So if Amelia changed what she said when she is upset and instead of saying 'I don't know' she started saying 'Please stop talking' you would probably stop talking."

"Of course." They turned to Amelia. "We just want to help you with this."

"That would give you some time to calm down before figuring this whole thing out, wouldn't it?" I asked Amelia.

"It's just too much."

"Amelia, let's spend a few minutes talking about some of the differences in the way you use language and communication. Understanding those differences is going to help you feel less anxious and upset. Is that okay with you?"

Amelia nodded. "I am so tired of getting upset."

"Okay then. Let's start with your strengths. I'm going to write them on a list while we talk. You have an excellent vocabulary and love to read. What else?"

Amelia thought for a minute. "I enjoy talking about things that interest me."

Her mother joined in, smiling. "It's hard to get you to stop talking sometimes!"

"And I'm guessing you remember a lot of details about things you've seen or read and can talk about those details," I added.

Amelia confirmed this.

"Now let's talk about some differences in the way you use language and communication. I noticed that you are a careful thinker who needs a little extra time to answer when other people are talking to you."

Patricia added, "Amelia's testing consistently shows that her processing speed is slower than her understanding of things. We forget that because she has such a great vocabulary and can talk at length about so many things."

"Yes, that can be confusing." I turned back to Amelia. "So instead of saying that you have a slow processing speed let's describe how it is for you: thinking carefully, taking your time."

"I like that," Patricia said. Amelia and Trevor nodded in agreement.

"Another difference I noticed is that you use more language, more details, more animation when you are in charge of the topic. Do you think that's the case?"

Amelia thought about this. "Yes, that's a fact. My friend George—he's a brony—is always telling me I want to do all the talking. And by the way, a brony is a teenager or adult who likes 'My Little Pony' in case you were wondering."

Trevor groaned.

"At the same time, when other people are in charge of the topic it looks like it's more of a struggle for you to answer and to talk using as much detail," I said.

"That's correct," Amelia confirmed.

"I also noticed that you have a distinctive way of speaking. You are sort of 'matter of fact' about things."

"And I like to correct people too, just ask my parents."

She thought a little more. "And speaking of my parents, sometimes they say things or use expressions and I have absolutely no idea what they are talking about. I don't have much patience for a lot of talk unless the topic is something I'm interested in. That's part of what bothers me at school. Except for George and Elissa everyone just wants to blather on about social stuff."

"So you prefer conversations about topics that interest you and don't like to have conversations about 'social stuff.'"

I introduced the concept of brain style at this point in the conversation.

"Amelia, as we've been talking about your strengths and differences in the way you use language and communication, we've been talking about your brain style. That is, the way your brain organizes information about language. Understanding your brain style gives us clues about the best ways to help you manage the aspects of communication that are hard work for you."

Amelia nodded once. "Like having my parents not talk so much."

"Exactly."

We continued our discussion as we finished the list for Amelia's Language and Communication Brain Style Profile.

"As we look at this list that describes your differences in language and communication—your brain style—it makes a lot of sense that sometimes you become upset when the conversation is started by other people or when too many questions are asked or the topic isn't focused on facts," I observed.

Patricia made a keen observation. "So maybe all these years Amelia's differences in her development have resulted in anxiety and depression? That makes so much more sense because Amelia is not constantly anxious or depressed but rather happy a lot of the time."

"Would you agree with that very thoughtful observation, Amelia?" I asked.

"I would! How about you, Dad?"

Trevor looked deep in thought. "Yes, I agree. This makes much more sense."

The Therapy Process with Amelia and Her Parents

Let's discuss the therapy process for Amelia and her parents. Prior to the initial family session Amelia's parents provided detailed information through the parent interview document about their concerns, Amelia's areas of preferred interest, and their goals for the therapy process. Their written interview recounted the history of their struggles to help their daughter regulate her anxiety as well as the challenges in helping her manage her pronounced sensory sensitivities and sensory-seeking routines. Their focus for our therapeutic conversation was on answering the question that had been posed by Amelia's previous therapist: Did Amelia have a form of autism?

- Each family member entered the therapy room communicating hesitation to engage yet again in the therapy process. Starting the conversation about Amelia's areas of interest through the entry point of commenting on her socks signaled to this family that the session was about inviting Amelia to talk about her interests, not about her struggles. Many children and adolescents with autism spectrum brain style differences bring visual clues into the session about their areas of passionate interest, in the form of clothing, books, or toys. In Amelia's case it was her My Little Pony socks. Noticing and commenting on her socks communicated to the family that this conversation was about Amelia's interests. Amelia notably alerted and engaged in the conversation and her autism spectrum worldview clearly unfolded in the initial portion of the session.
- Starting with Amelia's area of passionate interest established her as an expert. If her parents had been invited to start the session by sharing the existing family narrative—their area of expertise—Amelia would have withdrawn and experienced another uncomfortable and unpleasant conversation. It would have been much more difficult to establish her participation later in the session. Starting the session in this way can be thought of as entering into the autism conversation with the adolescent.
- Once Amelia's autism narrative had been established, her parents were invited to share their expertise. This took the form of reporting their daughter's areas of struggle. It allowed for an assessment of what this family conversation looked like. As Patricia and Trevor became alert and engaged in the conversation about their daughter's stress triggers, and as they prompted Amelia to share her narrative about her struggle, Amelia's reactivity became readily apparent. Things escalated quickly.

- Interrupting the familiar family communication cycle was necessary when it became apparent that Amelia was unable to process incoming information and she began pounding on her thigh. The directive *"stop talking"* had to be given in a firm and decisive way to interrupt the routine this family had established when discussing the topic of Amelia's anxiety and depression.
- Once the routine had been demonstrated and interrupted, it was important to begin the reframing process using descriptive language. Overtly commenting on the autism communication patterns gave Amelia and her parents a novel way to understand her communication process. Examples of this include noticing the difference in Amelia's language when she is talking versus listening (*"So when Amelia is talking about her beloved ponies she is picking the topic and you are listening."*) and framing her language processing challenges as the need to think carefully before answering (*"So I'm guessing when other people, like your parents, start asking you questions sometimes there is not enough time to think about your answer before they ask another question."*).
- Reframing her reactivity was also helpful, as it moved the historical experience of her emotional challenges from being about her to being about using different parts of her brain (*"It looks like when your parents ask you questions you go from the thinking part of your brain to the reacting part and it makes it really hard to talk or to listen to others talk."*). This reframing externalized her reactivity; a new way of thinking for Amelia and her parents.
- When adolescents with autism spectrum brain style differences become reactive they oftentimes use language that is unclear or that does not accurately represent what they are trying to communicate. In Amelia's case, her litany of *"I don't know"* was really trying to communicate *"stop talking."*
- Rather than directly stating to the family that Amelia was presenting a profile of behaviors consistent with a diagnosis of Autism Spectrum Disorder, they were introduced to the autism spectrum narrative through the process of identifying, describing, and chronicling Amelia's communication differences and constructing her Brain Style Profile. This process led in a natural way to a discussion about the diagnosis. After the Brain Style Profile is constructed the diagnosis has a context for the adolescent and the parents.
- In many cases, having this conversation with the parents and the adolescent together in the session works very well. It allows you to work simultaneously on framing the adolescent's autism spectrum differences while modeling conversational style and pacing to fit the adolescent's style and pace. It allows you to help the parents and the adolescent experience the narrative shift together. Sometimes meeting

with the adolescent and the parents separately is the best fit. As is always the case with family therapy, the clinician is the most helpful when carefully observing the family style and meeting the family at the natural entry point.

BOX 9.1 AMELIA'S BRAIN STYLE PROFILE

Language and Communication

Strengths:

Solid language skills;
Excellent vocabulary;
Loves to read and recalls details;
Enjoys talking about things that interest her.

Differences:

Even though her language skills are highly developed, incoming language is a source of stress for her;
Careful thinker; needs extra time before answering;
More animated, uses more details, talks more on self-selected topics of interest;
More of a struggle when other people are in charge of the topic;
Distinctive way of speaking; factual;
Corrects others frequently in conversation;
Low interest in and tolerance for social conversations with peers;
Sometimes does not follow what others are talking about;
Has to be reminded at times to include her conversational partner.

Strategies to Reduce Anxiety and Frustration Triggered in the Area of Language and Communication:

Practice using a "placeholder" in conversations ("give me a minute"; "let me see");
"Please stop talking for a minute" to regroup;
Observe and discuss observations of social conversations with peers to "break the code" and learn to participate in social conversations as needed;
Practice having conversations on topics selected by a conversational partner.

Developing the Autism Spectrum Narrative with Ian and His Parents

What would the application of narrative concepts and themes look like in a therapy session with an adolescent with autism spectrum differences who has already received the diagnosis? Ian's initial session with his parents provides an example of how to approach these key elements when the adolescent already has a diagnosis but has not yet developed a way to think about autism differences in a singular way.

"We don't know what else to do; since he started high school Ian misses at least one day of school every week. He refuses to get up and go." Miriam, Ian's mother, sat upright in her chair. She radiated tension and frustration. Her 14-year-old son sat with his head lowered, his elbows resting heavily on his knees. He held a thick paperback book in one hand. Ian's father, David, sat with his feet and arms crossed as he listened to his wife and watched his son.

"We'll definitely talk about that in a little bit," I said. I paused before addressing Ian directly. "May I ask what book you're reading, Ian?"

Ian lifted his wrist, exposing the cover of the book. A dragon, flames, and a sword figured prominently along with a one-word title.

"Looks like it's part of a series."

"This is the third book." Ian offered this fact as he engaged in conversation with me.

I noticed a tissue stuck in between the pages.

"Nice bookmark."

Ian expelled a puff of air in acknowledgement of my comment. He shifted his body posture slightly towards me in anticipation of my next comment or question.

Prior to our meeting, Ian's parents completed a detailed interview questionnaire that included information about their son's preferred interests and activities. As a result, I knew that Ian enjoyed reading fantasy book series and nonfiction books that dealt with string theory and physics.

"Your parents told me you are interested in string theory and physics as well." I paused before adding a comparison question. "So, what are your thoughts about string theory versus M-theory?"

Ian's posture indicated a notable increase in alertness when this topic was introduced. He took a moment to organize his thoughts before he responded.

"Well, both are very interesting. String theory is the theory of everything and M-theory tries to unify superstring theory by bringing the eleven dimensions together." As he delivered this information Ian shot a glance over at me for the first time since the session began.

"I read that the M in M-theory can stand for different words," I replied.

"Yes, but I prefer the term M-theory, as opposed to talking about membrane, magic, or mystery."

"So you do a lot of reading. Do you generally have a book with you at all times?"

"Yes I do."

"So I'm wondering, Ian, if reading is not only something you enjoy doing but that it also helps you in some ways."

Ian was quiet for a moment as he thought about what I'd suggested.

"Maybe," he said.

"Would you like me to tell you more about what I was wondering about your reading?"

"Yes . . . maybe. . ." Ian stretched out the vowels as he enunciated the two words.

"Well, I'm guessing that maybe reading helps you block out certain unwanted thoughts and feelings?"

"Maybe . . . okay, I think so."

I paused to encourage Ian to elaborate on this.

"When I read it relaxes me."

"And I'm guessing that the whole school thing—getting ready in the morning, leaving the house, leaving the world of your books—is not relaxing for you."

"That would be a good guess."

David and Miriam had been listening closely to the conversation and as the topic of school was introduced David offered some information.

"You need to know that although Ian has a tremendously difficult time getting to school, once he arrives there he always manages to stay the whole day. He even gets some work done while he is there."

"So getting to school is the difficult part, Ian?" I asked him directly.

"Yes . . . maybe."

"Can you say more about what gets in the way for you?"

Ian took some time before answering. "Well, my stomach hurts, my head hurts, and I don't want to move."

Miriam added her observations. "It's true. Ian often has a headache and says that his stomach hurts. That's true when it's time to go to school and also when it's time to leave the house for other things."

I nodded as I looked at Miriam and then addressed Ian again. "So, Ian, is it possible that when your stomach hurts and your head hurts that maybe you are experiencing some anxious feelings at the same time?"

"I can tell you that yes, I have anxious feelings too."

"Since you are interested in physics and science, I can tell you that when people experience anxiety and stress their bodies produce stress hormones and they sometimes get headaches and stomachaches. So, do you think your stress level goes up more when you think about school or when you think about leaving the house?"

"Leaving the house. Which of course I have to do to go to school." Ian was now fully engaged in our discussion, even though he remained dependent on me to provide the structure and prompts to keep the conversation going.

"So let's see if we can describe your stress level in more detail." I drew a line on a sheet of paper. "On a scale of 1 to 10, with 10 being the worst level of stress and anxiety and 1 being calm and relaxed—like when you are reading a book—what level do you see yourself when you absolutely cannot get out of the door to go to school?" I wrote the numbers 1, 5, and 10 under the line.

Ian looked at the line. "I would say a 9."

I wrote the number 9 under the line. "Let's talk about some words to describe levels of stress or anxiety. You tell me when I get to a word that fits a level 9 or 10. Ready?"

Ian nodded.

"Nervous, scared, worried, dread . . . "

"That's it: *dread.*"

"So *dread* is the intensity of the stress you're feeling when you are at a level 9 or 10." I wrote the word "dread" under the two highest numbers. "What word best describes when you are at a level 5?"

"Anxious."

I wrote the word anxious on the page. "And the feeling you associate with being at level 1?"

"Calm." He thought for a moment. "And sometimes relaxed."

"Let's fill in the rest of the scale. The word that describes your stress at level 3?"

"Nervous."

"And level 7?"

"Very anxious. Unpleasant."

"So now your anxiety—your dread, your nervousness—are on this paper. And you told us that your anxiety gets triggered when you have to leave the house. But that doesn't always happen. That's interesting."

Ian took a moment and made an observation. "Well for me it has to do with the aggregate. Going to school one day can be okay but over time it builds up and I can't leave the house. It always makes me anxious but not always to the 9 or 10 level."

"That's an important observation, Ian. So when the aggregate builds up—and it sounds like that happens about once a week—describe what you do while you are at home during the school day."

"I read. Most of the day I read and the rest of the time I sleep. But mostly I read."

"So maybe on those days you recharge or restore your system by reading and resting. And when you are at home reading and resting you have a break from some of the things that are stressful and tiring for you."

"Yes . . . maybe."

"One of the things I've noticed in our conversation today Ian, is that you seem to be a careful thinker. That is, you are someone who takes some time to decide what you're going to say when you are listening to someone. Does that seem like it might be accurate?"

Miriam responded for her son while he was taking time to think of his response. "That is absolutely true about Ian. Sometimes he answers me an hour after I've made a comment and by then I've forgotten what I was talking about and have to stop and remember to make sense out of what he says."

"Would you agree, Ian?" I asked.

"Yes, that's right."

"What are your thoughts about this, David?" I asked his father.

"I was thinking that Ian and I are alike in that way. I prefer having time to think before I speak. You might say that his mother and I differ in that way."

Miriam made a snorting sound. "Yes, you might say that."

"So the men in the family are careful thinkers."

"And scientific thinkers too," Ian added. "My dad and I both like to watch Nova Science Now."

"Thank you for adding that fact, Ian. Now we're beginning to be able to put together a way to talk about how your brain works. Reading and learning about science are things you enjoy and where you have excellent skills."

"Math, too. Don't forget math. I am completing the equations in a calculus book in my free time."

"Wow; amazing. Yes, math, too. And you are a careful thinker who likes to take time to decide what he wants to say before speaking. You and your dad."

"But not my mom so much."

"Not your mom so much. So, Ian, I am wondering if it is taking you a lot of energy or effort to manage all of the conversations you have to have when you go to school. There's a lot of listening and answering and talking you have to do, correct?"

"Too much. It gives me a stomachache and a headache."

"What about being around the other students? How is that for you?"

"Too much. It gives me a stomachache and a headache. They talk too much."

"So incoming language and social demands wear you out? By incoming, I mean when other people are talking to you and you have to listen and decide on your answers?"

"That's exactly right."

"I've noticed something else about the way you think during our conversation today Ian. May I share my observations with you?"

"Yes."

"Well, it sounds like once you start doing something it can be hard to stop doing it and to shift your focus onto a different thing. In other words, it might be hard for your brain to move back and forth between topics or events with flexibility."

"That is for certain true about Ian," Miriam remarked. "One thing at a time for him, and he stays with his reading or whatever for a long time. It's really hard to interrupt him."

"What do you think about that idea, Ian?"

"I think that's right."

"So if incoming language and social demands are stressful and wear you out, and if once you start reading or you stay home it's hard to do anything else, then you have to take a day or so a week to get yourself recharged and ready to go back to school. Is that about right?"

"I don't really want to stay home and read all of the time, but it wears me out to go to school."

"So you don't want to stay home and read all of the time, but you haven't quite found a way to handle how much school wears you out—in an aggregate way—other than staying home and regrouping."

Ian nodded.

I placed his experience of anxiety into a scientific context to help him externalize the problem.

"Would you be interested in doing an experiment to test out a possible alternative to your current pattern of managing stress?"

"I would be interested, yes."

"Well, to start with, let's not worry right now about trying to have you go to school more often. Let's gather some information so you can learn more about how your brain works and what it needs. Agreed?"

Ian looked at his parents and they nodded in agreement with each other. He turned to me as the spokesperson for the family. "Agreed."

"So, Ian, I want you to think about monitoring your stress level at different times during the day using the scale we just developed. That will give you information about how much stress you feel and how much range you have on the scale of stress during the day."

Ian turned to his father. "Dad, maybe we could chart this together using the graphics program?"

His father smiled and agreed that this would be a great idea.

"And to help you learn more about how flexible your brain can be, I suggest practicing a pattern of reading, then stopping, then reading, then stopping. In other words, read for short bursts and then try to concentrate on schoolwork or other activities. Record your stress level after each reading break so you can learn how much reading helps you recharge and gives you energy."

"So, back and forth instead of read, read, read?"

"Exactly."

It was time to end our first family session, I asked Ian and his parents to take a moment and tell me what they would be taking home from the session.

Ian went first. "I understand the connection between my stomachaches and headaches and my stress level better. I like the plan to graph my stress level."

"For me, as his mother, I learned that Ian actually would like to go to school but that the transition out of the house is difficult for him. Well, I already knew that it was difficult for him but now I have a better idea of why. And I feel hopeful because he talked with you and now we have a plan."

"I learned that Ian needs some practice training his brain to be flexible. I look forward to working with Ian to make his graphs too."

The Therapy Process with Ian and His Parents

Ian, Miriam, and David participated in the process of creating an alternative narrative for Ian regarding his anxiety and resistance to attending school. The mood and tone in the family became notably less weighty and gloomy as they were guided to change their autism story. Both of his parents alerted and engaged when new ways of thinking about their son were introduced. Ian became active in discussing the previously unpleasant topic of his reduced school attendance.

- Starting with Ian's areas of interest was a key step to engage him in the narrative process. Framing his anxiety as a scientific experiment and externalizing it in the visual schematic helped Ian separate from the problem. Separating the problem in this way allowed Ian to consider alternate stories and ways to understand himself and his autism spectrum brain differences.
- Gathering the parent interview narrative document prior to the initial session with the family gives you an opportunity to research key terms related to the adolescent's area of preferred interest. In Ian's case I was able to look up information about string theory and M-theory. This ability to introduce key terms signals to the adolescent with autism spectrum differences that you speak their language.
- Having the conversation with Ian placed him in the role of expert. It freed his parents from their role of constantly trying to "fix" their son and they were able to listen to Ian's insights in a new way. When Ian was invited into the conversation at the start of the session rather than his parents receiving the invitation, the result was his more active engagement in the problem-solving process ("*We'll definitely talk about that in a little bit. May I ask what book you're reading, Ian?*").
- Framing his somatic symptoms in a scientific way externalized his experience and opened the door to analyzing the essential components of his dilemma. The link between incoming language, social, and environmental demands and his somatic experience of headaches and stomachaches was now understood as a scientific equation. This led to the development of his anxiety rating scale and the plan to systematically collect data.

- Providing Ian with word choices was important. As is the case with many adolescents with autism spectrum brain style differences, Ian was better able to identify feelings that were a fit for him when he was given word choices than if he had been asked to generate the words independently. In Ian's case, he had a nuanced understanding of his range of anxiety but lacked the ability to articulate these nuances without support. With support, he was able to make the key point that anxiety about leaving the house is a cumulative process for him ("*Well for me it has to do with the aggregate. Going to school one day can be okay but over time it builds up and I can't leave the house. It always makes me anxious but not always to the 9 or 10 level.*").
- Creating the document of the scale in the session led to Ian inviting his father to work with him to create a scale using a graphics computer program. This led to a discussion about how Ian and David share thinking style traits ("*I was thinking that Ian and I are alike in that way. I prefer having time to think before I speak.*").
- The role reading plays for Ian was discussed as a functional behavior ("*So you don't want to stay home and read all of the time but you haven't quite found a way to handle how much school wears you out—in an aggregate way—other than staying home and regrouping.*").
- Ian had a long-standing routine of becoming overwhelmed with the pressure to increase his school attendance. It was important to directly state that the immediate goal was not to increase his school attendance but to gather more information ("*Well to start with, let's not worry right now about trying to have you go to school more often. Let's gather some information so you can learn more about how your brain works and what it needs. Agreed?*").
- The concept of training brain flexibility was introduced and placed within the context of an experiment with his reading. This was linked to Ian's recording of his stress levels ("*So, back and forth instead of read, read, read?*").
- Ending the session by inviting each family member to express the main points each would be taking from the session reinforces the family narrative of mastery and competence.

Notes

1 McLaughlin, Sharon, and Rafferty, Harry (2015). "Me and 'It:' Seven Young People Given a Diagnosis of Asperger's Syndrome." In *Autism and Education, Volume 1: Key Perspectives and Themes in Autism Education*. New York, NY: Sage Publications.
2 Gould, Judith, and Ashton-Smith, Jacqui (2011). "Missed Diagnosis or Misdiagnosed? Girls and Women on the Autism Spectrum." *Good Autism Practice*, Volume 12, Number 1, pages 34–48. British Institute of Learning

Disabilities; Attwood, Tony (2008). *The Complete Guide to Asperger's Syndrome.* London, England: Jessica Kingsley Publisher; Nichols, Shanna (2009). *Girls Growing Up on the Autism Spectrum: What Parents and Professionals Should Know About the Pre-Teen and Teenage Years.* London, England: Jessica Kingsley Publisher.

10 Young Adults

Moving the Family Story Forward

- Place the individual's autism spectrum differences in the context of universal young adult developmental tasks.
- Shape the narrative from the language of limitations to the language of possibilities within the scope of the individual's singular presentation of autism brain style differences.
- Help parents define their changing narrative as it relates to their young adult child.

Supporting the Development of Emotional Resiliency and Coping Skills

- Support the development of a vocabulary to describe and express emotions.
- Teach the young adult to recognize and manage sensory thresholds.
- Encourage the development of a self-determination and self-advocacy narrative.

Identifying and Managing the Autism Spectrum Brain Style

- Support the development of the narrative of the young adult's style as it relates to autism spectrum differences, highlighting areas of strength as well as differences.
- Help the individual match sensory needs and interests with compatible work and social environments.
- Introduce the narrative of learning through experiences to replace the narrative of failure.

The transition from adolescence to young adulthood is a transformative time for all families. Parents and their young adult children go through a period of instability and flux, as roles are renegotiated and redefined. As a clinician, you play an important part in supporting families. You help families move their stories forward.

Key developmental tasks form the core of this stage in the life cycle, leading to the emergence of the individual's adult identity.[1] The pursuit of interests, school, work, sexuality, and significant relationships outside of the family are all part of the young adult process of exploration and transformation. These universal developmental tasks are very much a part of this process for young adults with autism spectrum differences. They are launching from their families, but in many cases they are doing so with different parameters than the circumstances of their typically developing counterparts. Part of the therapy process is helping young adults and their parents define the launching process in developmental terms that are a fit for their individual autism story.

For families with young adults on the autism spectrum, the narrative of limitations can loom large at this stage. Many individuals with autism spectrum differences continue to require substantial support from their families as they mature into adulthood. Some individuals graduate from high school and face an uncertain future without the established school supports in place. Access to peers becomes more challenging to arrange, resulting in isolation, and in some situations, in a loss of previously mastered social competencies. Many individuals have the intellectual ability to make the transition to college and work but have not yet acquired the necessary social skills and awareness level to successfully navigate life separate from their families. The natural uncertainty that is a part of daily life for families as their adolescent makes the passage into young adulthood is magnified for parents whose child has autism spectrum brain style differences.

A major therapy task in working with young adults involves supporting the development of emotional resiliency and coping skills.[2] Young adults with autism spectrum differences often experience significant anxiety and depression.[3] The predictable structure of daily life at school drops off, leaving large amounts of time to structure and fill. Natural opportunities to interact with same-age peers become less available and this sometimes leads to a pattern of withdrawal from new situations, as the person with autism spectrum differences avoids the anxiety associated with social interactions. This cycle further isolates the young person. The logistics of arranging for job interviews, securing a job, managing the details involved in a job, or enrolling for college classes, attending classes, completing assignments, and managing the relationships with professors and classmates are oftentimes experienced as overwhelming. Stasis sets in and the young adult stays at home, oftentimes becoming increasingly absorbed in sensory pursuits such as online gaming, reading, or sleeping. Conflict between the young adult and his or her parents can intensify at this stage, as each family member is faced with redefining roles. Communication patterns that worked during adolescence are no longer a good fit during this next stage in the life of the family.

Therapy that supports the young adult's development of a vocabulary to describe and express emotions is important for young adults on the autism spectrum. Equally important, therapy provides the young adult with the necessary support to learn to recognize and manage the person's sensory thresholds. How much is too much? As the young adult with autism spectrum differences gains the vocabulary to express emotions and to recognize and manage his or her sensory threshold needs, a sense of competency and emotional resiliency emerges.

Within the scope of the individual's singular presentation of autism brain style differences, clinicians support families in moving their story forward by shaping the narrative from the language of limitations to the language of possibilities. Maybe the young adult is not ready to make the transition to living away from home. Naturally, parents experience this as a limitation. But within the boundaries of the young adult's current abilities, introducing the language of possibilities changes the conversation. Within the limitation of living at home, many possibilities emerge. Small steps forward in the autonomy process for the young adult can be identified and recognized for the achievements they represent.

Working directly with young adults, separate from their parents, provides the necessary structure to support the development of their distinctive personal narrative. As you help the young adult develop his or her singular story, organized around style and strengths, you support the identity of self-determination. Individual therapy with young adults on the autism spectrum provides the young adult with the necessary language to describe his or her goals, talents, and needs. This is a crucial step in supporting the individual's ability to advocate for his or her needs with the significant people in his or her life. When self-determination and self-advocacy form the central focus of the autism conversations with young adults and their parents the family is able to move their story forward.

So how does one go about supporting the development of self-determination and self-advocacy skills? What goes into the shaping of an empowered personal narrative?

Conversations with the young adult that focus on helping the person identify his or her autism spectrum brain style provides the foundation for the singular narrative. Identifying brain style characteristics leads to a discussion of ways for that person to manage his or her brain style differences. Issues to discuss with young adults include helping the person match his or her sensory needs and interests with compatible work, school, and social environments. Many young adults with autism spectrum differences experience failure and are at risk of having failure form the core of their self-identity. Clinicians can help the individual disengage from this central failure identity through the introduction of the narrative of learning through experiences. Experiences provide important information. When the young adult is guided through a process of applying this narrative, the conversation shifts from one of recounting failures to deconstructing the elements of the experience. The conversation can then focus on helping the individual view the revisiting of the experience as an opportunity to extract information that will lead to making future empowered decisions.

Parents of young adults on the autism spectrum benefit from separate therapy sessions as well. This life stage brings many anxieties and worries to the forefront for parents, as their child is now an adult who continues to require substantial support. As parents age they are oftentimes dealing with their own challenges. There is more of a sense of urgency to equip their child with independence skills, as the reality sets in that the parents will not be there forever to take care of their adult child. When their sense of urgency comes face-to-face with the reality of their young adult's apparent lack of awareness of the importance of accomplishing daily tasks, it is difficult for parents to see things from the perspective of their young adult child. It is difficult for them to change the way they think about their child and the way they communicate. Changing the conversation in the therapy sessions with the parents is an important part of working with young adults with autism spectrum differences.

Family therapy conversations with the young adult and his or her parents are also vitally important, as the joint sessions provide a structured place to help each family member process the impact of this life cycle stage while redefining and renegotiating their changing roles.

Leland and His Parents Move Their Family Story Forward

Leland, a tall 22-year-old young man with pronounced dark eyebrows and wavy hair, walked with a purposeful stride as he entered the room. His torso was extended slightly in front of the rest of his body and, as was his custom, he was wearing a colorful t-shirt with graphics of the Despicable Me Minions characters on the front. He carried a folded sheet of paper containing his typed list of topics to discuss during our session.

Leland and his family had been working with me since early adolescence. He had a long-standing diagnosis of Autism Spectrum Disorder (Asperger's Syndrome was his original diagnosis), and his interest in all things related to Universal Studios and their Theme Parks remained an enthusiastic and integral part of his life. His ultimate goal in life was to work at a Universal Studios Theme Park. Leland had an excellent memory for information related to actors, directors, animators, characters, and movie plots, and enjoyed sharing his passionate interest with others. Conversations that involved other topics were a bit more challenging for Leland, but he was an exceptionally good-natured and agreeable person who worked hard at participating in activities with others. Although he required extra thinking time to gather his thoughts, Leland consistently added thoughtful comments to the therapy conversations.

With some accommodations and supports, Leland was in the process of completing his college degree. He had learned to drive a car and was able to independently travel to and from necessary places, such as home to school and to his part-time job at the movies. He had not yet established genuine friendships with same-age peers and depended on his parents for companionship. Leland was beginning to show an interest in talking about and gaining the necessary skills to start forming relationships with other young adults. In our sessions together I helped Leland develop a plan for identifying one or two peers with whom he might want to have a conversation, the steps involved in starting a conversation, and in keeping it going.

Early on in our work together, Leland and his parents gained an understanding of his brain style differences. When it was time for Leland to apply for his part-time job, stocking shelves and sacking groceries in a neighborhood store, we worked on preparing a list of "5 things my employer needs to know about me." Leland scheduled a meeting with the manager, interviewed for the job, and was hired. He was a highly reliable and productive worker. When something bothered him at work, such as being told he needed to work a longer shift and not clock out according to his predetermined schedule, Leland talked about it with his parents and in his therapy sessions. A visual checklist was created to provide Leland with a plan to follow "when something unexpected happens." The use of visual supports helped Leland manage his anxiety and he continued to gain work experience.

Leland's parents, Margaret and Brooks, worked diligently to provide their son with the support he needed to increasingly gain functional independence. We had several therapy sessions without Leland present, where they discussed their worries about his social challenges. Leland expressed a desire for friendships but had not yet found peers who shared his interests. Leland's interests were those of a much younger person. He was literal in his understanding of the world and had a strong sense of wrong and right. One of their main concerns was his inflexibility at home. Although Leland was functioning well at school and at work, when he was at home he had episodes of intense anger, with shouting, arguing, and refusing to disengage. These were almost always triggered by Leland's perception that something had not gone as planned or that his parents had gone back on their word. Margaret and Brooks worried that Leland would never gain control over his reactivity. They worried that he would be at risk for others taking advantage of him.

Leland worked with me to develop his self-regulation tools. Over the course of several months, he went from feeling like he was "being sucked into the dark vortex of depression and rage" to "I get angry but when I cool down I can tell others what is bothering me." His parents confirmed this milestone in Leland's development.

In our most recent session, Leland talked about being bothered by the way his parents talked to him. Specifically, he was beginning to notice that his parents continued to base their communication with him on reminding him what to do and asking him to do things. From Leland's perspective, they were continuing to treat him like a child. This was not a good fit with his growing identity as a man.

Let's join Leland and his parents in their session together.

Leland sat with his typed sheet on his lap. He faced his parents, who looked at him expectantly.

"There is something on my mind that I want to talk about. Just because I still love movies and cartoons doesn't mean I'm still a child. You are still treating me like I was ten years old." Leland did not waste any time getting to his point.

Brooks spoke first. "Leland, we recognize that you are an adult, not a child. But sometimes you still act like a child."

"I do not! I am an adult!" Leland lowered his formidable eyebrows.

"Can you give us some examples of how you think we still treat you like a child?" Margaret entered the conversation.

Leland extended one last glare at his father before he gathered his thoughts and responded to his mother's question.

"Both of you: All you ever do is tell me what to do, or remind me of what I haven't done yet, or ask me to do something." He placed his right hand lightly on his t-shirt, tapping the graphic of the yellow cartoon figures wearing goggles and blue overalls. "I may be like Mark, Lance, and Dave, and it is true, that I am fiercely loyal to the two of you, just like the Minions are to Felonious Gru, but the fact is, I am now a man and not a kid."

Brooks and Margaret listened attentively to their son. Brooks responded. "You're right, Leland. You are a man. Sometimes we forget that. We apologize."

"And you're right; we do spend a lot of time reminding you to do things. I hadn't really noticed how we've slipped into that pattern." Margaret observed. "It's just that we want you to be able to keep up with everything. We're just trying to help you."

Leland nodded.

"Well, you do help me and I appreciate that. But that's all you do. You never talk about anything else. Every time you talk to me you remind me about what I haven't done yet."

"I guess that's because we worry about you, son. We want to help you continue to make progress," Brooks said.

Leland lowered his eyebrows once again.

"It's a lot of pressure! I don't like it."

"Leland, can you talk with your parents about some of the things they used to have to help you with but that you do on your own now?" I prompted Leland to stay regulated and focused on his areas of success.

Leland sighed and looked off to one side as he thought about this request. He directed his gaze back to his parents. He lifted his index finger and added a finger each time he added an item to his list.

"I can drive myself where I need to go. I get myself up and ready for work or school in the morning without your reminders. I go to class. I go to work. Oh, and I cook my own macaroni and cheese."

His parents nodded as Leland recited his list of independent activities.

"You're right; we forget to appreciate all of the independent things you do that you used to need our help with. I guess we are in the habit of pushing you to do more. Like put your dishes in the sink and remember to feed Patches and brush your teeth. . ."

"I get it, I get it, Mom! That is exactly my point!"

I directed my next observation to Margaret and Brooks. "You have worked so hard to help your son, and he has accomplished so much. The habit of reminding and pushing served a good purpose. But now that Leland is able to do so many things independently, what is he telling you he needs from you?"

Brooks replied in a thoughtful tone. "You know, Leland, we've been so busy trying to teach you things that we haven't taken the time to just talk about things. Is that what you're telling us?"

Leland nodded emphatically. "Yes! You never want to talk about movies and I want to tell you stuff."

Brooks nodded. "We used to talk about movies more. We can do that now."

Leland took his father literally.

"Well as a matter of fact, I just discovered that the voice for Jerry the Minion is a New Zealand actor called Jemaine Clement. And he was in a show called Flight of the Conchords with Bret MacKenzie, who wrote the Oscar-winning song for the Muppets movie."

"Wow, I didn't know that, Leland," his father replied. He quickly continued before Leland could share more movie details. "What I meant, Leland, was that we need to plan some time when we are home together to talk about and watch movies together. Would you like that?"

"That would be great!" He turned to his mother. "Mom? You, too?"

Margaret nodded and smiled. "Me, too."

Leland consulted his list.

"And another thing. Dad, sometimes you do not treat me with the respect that I deserve. For example, when I was upset about Patrick's making fun of me when he was home from college last month, you told me: 'Get over it, Leland, you just need to deal with your brother when he is playing around.'" His eyebrows lowered and his voice volume increased as he recalled the incident. "Patrick was inappropriate and I do not appreciate it when you tell me to 'deal with it.'"

Brooks was about to speak, but Leland was not finished.

"You have to remember that some things are harder for me, like going along with inappropriate joking, and that is something that is part of my brain difference. I am learning how to deal with things that bother me and although I do still become quite angry at times, like right now, I can handle myself and not do anything regrettable." Leland continued to scowl but remained in control, making his point with clarity.

"Well said, Leland. And you're right. I apologize," Brooks said.

Leland's scowl evaporated. "And I accept your apology."

Margaret spoke up, her voice filled with emotion. "Leland, I am so proud of you for telling us what you've been thinking and feeling. You handled that like the exceptional young man that you are."

"Thank you, Mom. Now maybe we can talk about something else."

The Therapy Process with Leland and His Parents

Leland's goal for the session with his parents was to assert his emerging identity as a young adult. Prior to the session with his parents, Leland worked with me to help him organize his thoughts and to prepare himself for this important conversation.

- Leland and his parents benefited from their individual sessions prior to the family session. During his separate sessions, Leland was able to experience working on his goals in a setting where he was comfortable, without his parents. This experience helped him develop a sense of his emerging adult identity. He was able to work on the development of social and emotional regulation skills. He was able to talk about what bothered him about his communication patterns with his parents. The structure of the sessions followed a set routine, as Leland prepared his list prior to each meeting. His lists always contained one or two incidences in his life that were bothering him and our sessions began with a discussion of strategies to deal with those challenges. The strategies were outlined in a list generated during the session. Each time, Leland would work hard for the bulk of the session time. When he reached his threshold for absorbing information, Leland made the statement: "*Now maybe we can talk about something else.*" He followed this statement with a quick consultation with his prepared list and shared new facts about his preferred topic. At the end of each session, Leland was able to verbally summarize the two or three key points or strategies from the meeting.
- During their sessions, Margaret and Brooks were able to speak candidly about their worries and concerns for their son without the added burden of worrying about how he would interpret what they said. Practical details, such as coaching Leland to practice his

interview multiple times prior to going in for the interview for his job, and guiding him through the step-by-step process of enrolling for his classes online and setting up his organizational agenda to keep track of his coursework, were discussed with his parents as well. These sessions helped them build their skills in continuing to provide Leland with the step-by-step supports he needed while handing over more responsibility to him. Leland's perception that his parents were telling him what to do was inextricably linked to the shift his parents were making from doing things for Leland to prompting Leland to do things independently.

- During their family session, Leland was able to experience advocating for himself by preparing for the session in advance, having his list of topics available, and starting the conversation with his parents (*"There is something on my mind that I want to talk about."*).
- Leland became reactive when his father responded to Leland's initial, prepared statement by telling Leland he acted like a child. His mother redirected the conversation back to Leland's point (*"Can you give us some examples of how you think we still treat you like a child?"*).
- Leland required additional time and preparation to address substantive issues and became reactive when his conversational partners made statements that did not fit his expectations. Both Leland and his parents needed practice in the therapy setting to learn how to have substantive conversations.
- After his initial comment about his son's childish behavior, Brooks made the shift to treating Leland's concerns in a serious and age-congruent way (*"You're right, Leland. You are a man. Sometimes we forget that. I apologize."*). This correction in their communication—from father/child to father/young man—reinforced Leland's emerging young adult identity (*"I may be like Mark, Lance, and Dave, and it is true, that I am fiercely loyal to the two of you, just like the Minions are to Felonious Gru, but the fact is, I am now a man and not a kid."*).
- Leland was in the process of learning to recognize and manage his reactivity without becoming overly agitated. He was becoming reactive to his father's comments about continuing to make progress, and was able to use words to communicate his agitation (*"It's a lot of pressure! I don't like it."*). It was apparent, though, that his limited resources were approaching his threshold. I provided a specific prompt to redirect Leland, and to place him back in charge of the conversation with his parents (*"Leland, can you talk with your parents about some of the things they used to have to help you with but that you do on your own now?"*).
- Leland practiced self-determination by listing all of his accomplishments.
- Margaret was consistently able to tell her son that she appreciated his achievements. However, both Margaret and Brooks had established

a routine with Leland that paired a comment of acknowledgement of his young adult independence with a comment about his areas of dependency (*"I guess we are in the habit of pushing you to do more. Like put your dishes in the sink and remember to feed Patches and brush your teeth . . ."*). I acknowledged that routine and the good purpose it had served before redirecting the conversation back to Leland's main point (*"But now that Leland is able to do so many more things independently, what is he telling you he needs from you?"*).

- Leland was able to tell his parents what he needed from them. His father summed it up well, addressing his son as an adult rather than as a child (*"You know, Leland, we've been so busy trying to teach you things that we haven't taken the time to just talk about things. Is that what you're telling us?"*).

- They were able to make a plan to have conversations about movies at home.

- Leland exercised his autonomy and renegotiated his relationship with his father when he brought up the way his father spoke with him when his brother was making fun of him (*"Patrick was inappropriate and I do not appreciate it when you tell me to 'deal with it.'"*).

- Leland was able to finish his statement before waiting for a response from his father. This experience, of being in a setting where he had time before the conversation to organize and practice expressing his thoughts, and had a structured place where he knew he would have the opportunity to express his statements without being interrupted, was vitally important for Leland.

- Brooks genuinely listened to his son and took responsibility for his words without sidetracking the conversation into explanations or justifications. Leland's positive response was immediate.

- Without a doubt, the session represented the most sustained conversation Leland had had with his parents. He advocated for himself, maintained control over his reactivity, and communicated the key points that were of serious importance to him.

- When his threshold had been reached for processing the substantive content of the conversation, Leland was able to clearly communicate that he was finished (*"Now maybe we can talk about something else."*).

Becca and Her Development of Emotional Resiliency and Coping Skills

"Failure is not an option."

Becca made this declarative statement as we began talking about her recent episode of highly agitated behavior at home, triggered by her thwarted attempt to get her crafts (sewing stuffed animals and costumes), and her computer to cooperate with her. Becca, a 20-year-old young woman, was living with her parents and attending college classes. Each time Becca came in for a session she wore a distinctive outfit. She loved cats and always had a Hello Kitty key chain attached to her purse. Many times she wore shirts or pants with animal prints. We had several animated conversations about whether to consider Hello Kitty as a cartoon of a girl or of a cat, with Becca firmly declaring that Hello Kitty is "actually the personification of a cat." Becca had named her own cat Charmmy Kitty, after Hello Kitty's pet cat.

Becca and I had worked together to help her develop her personal narrative and she had a good grasp on her brain style differences. She was working with her college's office of disabilities support services and was learning how to manage the organizational skills required to successfully complete her classes. She was in her second year of college and was on her way to earning her undergraduate degree. She was thinking of majoring in theater, as she enjoyed watching movies, going to see plays, crafting animals and costumes out of felt, and reading fiction. Sherlock Holmes, with his powerfully deductive mind, was one of her heroes.

An area that Becca and her parents were concerned about was her inability to manage her frustration when she was trying to complete a task and encountered challenges. She was highly reactive to this type of stress and had developed a rigid routine of swearing, yelling, and berating herself while refusing to leave the frustrating task to cool down and try again at a later time. When she was in a calm mental state Becca was resistant to attempts made by her parents to discuss her reactivity. Becca agreed, somewhat reluctantly at first, to work with me. When we met, Becca told me that she had worked with therapists when she was younger and in her recollection it had not been of much help to her. Her inflexible thinking was prominently displayed when she laid out her dilemma for me: "I should have learned how to handle my frustration by my age so now it's too late."

We worked through this no-win thinking by placing her inflexible thinking into her autism Brain Style Profile. Part of Becca's autism Brain Style Profile highlighted the fact that she was a "binary thinker," meaning that she tends to see things as "either/or." Binary thinking led to the inflexible rule of setting an age limit on acquiring this specific skill. Using this binary thinking framework provided a way to talk with Becca about new possibilities. Instead of following the "it's too late" rule, Becca was able to consider that the binary process of deciding to either do more of the same or do something different was worth exploring.

Let's join Becca in the session where she begins to apply the idea of doing something different.

"So Becca, when you say that 'failure is not an option,' tell me more about what you mean by that."

Becca considered this for a moment. "It's like this: I have the skill to do something but I get frustrated when I am not applying my skills to the standard necessary to get the job done. I am a very independent person and when I know I can do something I will NOT ask for help. So don't even think that that is a solution."

After listening to Becca I asked her if I could write some of this down to help us work through her situation, step-by-step.

"Great idea. That way we can use some deductive reasoning. Like you know who." Becca referenced the great Sherlock Holmes.

I wrote: "Failure is not an option" and "I have the skills but am not applying them to the standard necessary to get the job done."

"So it sounds like the triggers for your frustration are tasks that require skill. Would you say that's accurate?" I asked.

Becca gently rocked her head forward several times as she though it over. "That's correct. Also, postponing or putting off something that is hard for me is not allowed. I consider that giving up, which is failure, which is not an option."

I wrote: "Postponing something that is difficult = giving up" and showed it to Becca. She rocked her head in agreement.

I handed the page to Becca along with a pencil. "Becca, it's possible to change this rule. What if the old rule changed from 'postponing something that is difficult = giving up' to 'postponing something difficult does *not* equal giving up?' Can you change the equal sign to *not* equal?"

Becca considered this for a moment, the pencil poised over the equation. She raised her eyebrows, shrugged her shoulders, and drew a line through the equal sign. "You said I should try something different. Making these two things unequal is definitely different."

"So if postponing something difficult *is* allowed, tell me something you could do to feel better quickly."

Becca alerted her body. "Cat break! Cat break with Charmmy Kitty!"

"Excellent thinking! Cat break with Charmmy Kitty. Would you write down: 'cat breaks are allowed?' "

Becca wrote this down.

"So Becca, let's create a scale that shows your progression from 1 to 5, with a 1 being no worries and a 5 being when you are really frustrated."

Becca handed the notepad back to me. "You write and I'll think."

I used a new sheet of paper and drew a line with the numbers 1 through 5 underneath. "Let's talk about the best words to describe how you feel when you are at a level 1. The opposite of failure."

Becca thought aloud. "Let's see, the opposite of failure . . . skilled! Capable! Competent!"

"Wow, those are great descriptors, Becca." I wrote them under level 1. "And how do you feel when you are experiencing being skilled, capable, and competent?"

"In control. Good. Happy."

I wrote the descriptive words down. "Let's move up to level 5. Describe what level 5 is like."

Becca reflected for a moment and scowled. "Blowout . . . failure . . . upset."

"Blowout is a very descriptive word. So what would be the best way to describe what level 2 is like?"

"Well, at level 2 I'm not too frustrated yet but I do start to give myself directions inside."

I asked Becca to help me understand what she meant by that.

"I tell myself: 'put this in order,' and 'get this done.' I give myself directions to tell myself to do what it takes to get the job done."

"And the feelings you link to this level; when you are giving yourself directions?"

"It's more work and not fun anymore. I guess you would say I start to feel like I am working harder and maybe I'm getting nervous about getting things done up to my standard." Becca paused. "Hey, I just thought of something. My parents have told me this but I never thought it was true before. They tell me that I hold myself up to higher standards than what I expect from other people."

"That's an important point, Becca. So would you say you are harder on yourself than you are on other people?"

"Well, yes, other people can make mistakes because, well, they are flawed. Failure is not only an option but an inevitability. When other people make mistakes it's mildly annoying at times but I expect it to happen. I never expect it when I fail at something I know I can do."

I wrote: "give directions inside (put this in order, get this done)" under level 2.

Becca was ahead of me for level 3. "For level 3, I would say that things are getting frustrating. And things are getting cluttered or messy. Pins are everywhere, I can't find the piece of felt I need to make the part of the animal I'm making, or I can't find the website I'm looking for on the computer."

"So by level 3, Becca, would you say that you are still somewhat in control but that you are definitely starting to feel frustrated?"

"Yes. Definitely."

Under level 3, I wrote: "Things are getting cluttered or messy, I can't find things, I am somewhat in control but definitely frustrated."

Becca rocked her head again. "That leaves level 4." She gathered her thoughts. "Postponing is not an option! Things are getting really frustrating and difficult. Unhappy. Not good."

I wrote these descriptors under level 4.

"Great scale, Becca. Now you have a way to think about the whole range of experiences, from in control to blowout. This is a good example of how you are training your brain to expand your binary thinking."

"Hey! Now I can call myself an *incremental* thinker."

We both smiled and laughed at this witty description. "That's very funny. Becca. And true. So what do you think about this incremental scale?"

"I think it's good. I really was thinking at a level 1 or a level 5 without paying much attention to the increments."

"So if you were to set a goal of how far up this scale you want to try and keep yourself from going, what would you say is your top level?"

"Maybe a 3? I really hate the way I feel when I get to a 4 or 5."

"That's a great goal, Becca. It will help if you start a routine of doing a self-check when you are crafting or doing computer work so that you become more aware of your levels as you work."

"I can do that."

"So now we just need to talk about a plan and some options for you so that you can replace the upset routine with a calming routine." I started another page in the notepad. "When you are frustrated, your brain goes from thinking to reacting. So let's start a contrast list of what you say and do when you are reacting and when you are thinking." I wrote "reacting" on the top left-hand side of the page and "thinking" on the right-hand side. I drew a line separating the two columns.

"Well, when I am reacting I swear quite a bit. I yell and actually scream."

I wrote these descriptors under "reacting."

Becca continued. "And I scream, 'why?' and 'no excuses' and 'failure is not an option.'"

I wrote down the phrases as she dictated them. "Becca, those are very descriptive. I'm going to add a general category that all of those statements fall under. When you tell yourself all of those things you are being very critical of yourself. The word 'berate' comes to mind."

Becca rocked her head forward in agreement. "I do berate myself."

"And that berating is not working very well to help you get back over to the thinking part of your brain, is it?"

"No, it is not."

"So let's talk about things you can do and things you can tell yourself that will have a calming and soothing effect on you."

Becca alerted in the same way she had earlier in the session when she thought about Charmmy Kitty. "Cat break! Cat breaks are now allowed. I can go love Charmmy Kitty. I can never feel frustrated when I am with Charmmy Kitty."

"Great idea. And Charmmy Kitty will like that too. What does she do when you are screaming and berating yourself?"

"Oh, she darts under the furniture and waits until the storm passes. She'll be much happier if her mommy stays calm."

"Let's talk about some things you can tell yourself when you are at a level 2 or 3 so that you can practice soothing yourself and keep from escalating to a level 4 or 5. Think about what you might say to someone else if you were trying to encourage them."

Becca thought about this. "Well, I would say: 'everything's going to be fine.' I could also tell myself: 'taking a break is allowed' and 'taking a break is not giving up, it's the smart thing to do.'"

"Excellent. Those are great things to tell yourself. When you tell yourself those things you are staying in control. You are using your thinking part of your brain to solve a problem."

"Just like Sherlock Holmes. Solving problems." She paused for a moment. "Hey! I can tell my reacting part of my brain: 'I am Sherlock Holmes, not you!' "

"So true, Becca. I love that!" I added her comments to her "thinking" list.

It was time to end the session. "Becca, you did outstanding work in here today. What are your thoughts about the things we talked about?"

"I feel better because for the first time I have a plan that I can use to stop myself from getting so frustrated. I didn't think I would ever figure this out. Before, people were telling me to take deep breaths and to understand that I was making a big deal out of nothing but that really didn't help. I like my plan."

"Good. I'm happy to hear that. And I admire you for learning how to think more flexibly."

Becca interrupted me. "You mean, think more *incrementally*."

"Right, more *incrementally*." I handed the pages we had worked on to take with her. "What do you think about talking with your parents about your new strategies?"

"I can do that. If I tell them, they can help me. Now they just irritate me when I get frustrated."

The Therapy Process with Becca

Becca's long-standing emotional regulation challenge was the focus of the session. Her established narrative, "failure is not an option," was interfering with her ability to develop emotional resiliency and coping skills.

- Introducing the narrative of contrasting doing more of the same with doing something different worked well for Becca when it was placed in the context of her binary thinking brain style.
- Documenting Becca's declarative statements provided a visual way for her to see the narrative rules and restrictions she was placing on herself. It allowed for the introduction of alternative ways of viewing the rules (*"Can you change the equal sign to not equal?"*). Prompting her to draw the line through the equal sign emphasized the change in thinking for her.
- Introducing the regulation scale provided the framework to help Becca recognize the incremental steps that occurred when she began to escalate into her reactive state. Starting at the binary extremes (levels 1 and 5) and working through the in-between steps helped Becca identify her emotional and behavioral range and the clues that she was becoming dysregulated before a full-blown escalation occurred (*"Now you have a way to think about the whole range of experiences, from in control to blowout. This is a good example of how you are training your brain to expand your binary thinking."*).

- Once the scale was developed, asking Becca to set a target level reinforced the narrative of competence (*"So if you were to set a goal of how far up this scale you want to try and keep yourself from going, what would you say is your top level?"*).
- Using the binary chart that contrasted *"reacting"* with *"thinking"* helped Becca identify the tools she already had to self-regulate. This externalization of her reactivity allowed Becca to relate to being in the thinking part of her brain (*"Hey! I can tell my reacting part of my brain: 'I am Sherlock Holmes, not you!'"*).
- Encouraging Becca to review her plan with her parents emphasized her role as a young adult in charge of managing her emotional reactivity. This process of identifying strategies and having Becca tell her parents about her plan was an important part of her growing experience of emotional resiliency and coping skills.

Notes

1   Arnett, Jeffery Jensen (2014). *Emerging Adulthood: The Winding Road from the Late Teens Through the Twenties.* Oxford University Press.
2   Gaus, Valerie L., and Shore, Stephen (2011). *Living Well on the Spectrum: How to Use Your Strengths to Meet the Challenges of Asperger Syndrome/ High Functioning Autism.* Guilford Press.
3   Gaus, Valerie L. (2007). *Cognitive-Behavioral Therapy for Adult Asperger Syndrome.* Guilford Press.

Section IV

Therapy Resources

11 Organizational Supports

Visual Schedules

- Visual schedules support communication by "showing" while "telling."
- The child is better able to organize, retrieve, and use language to communicate when visual supports are linked to everyday activities.
- Parents and children make the shift from powerless to capable when a visual system is in place.

Step-by-Step Visual Maps

- Sequencing of events increases predictability when visual supports are used.
- Visual maps create routines.
- Visual maps support the shift from prompt-dependence to autonomy.

Organizational Systems

- Visually organizing the child's environment adds predictability.
- Visually organized systems signal: "how much and how long" demands will be placed on the child.
- Predictability and the use of systematic routines builds cognitive flexibility and supports the shift from dysregulated to controlled.

Visual Schedules

Visual schedules are a key resource for clinicians working with individuals with autism spectrum differences and their families. They can take many forms, from representational objects, to line drawings linked with key written words, to photographs, or written lists. The form of the visual schedule depends on the age and ability level of the child.

Why are visual schedules such an important organizational support for children with autism spectrum differences? Visual schedules support communication by providing a way to "show" what is being communicated while "telling." Children with autism spectrum brain style differences organize best with visual supports because they are visual thinkers. Listening to verbal directions without the support of corresponding visual contextual cues is hard work for many individuals with autism spectrum differences, resulting in an avoidance of verbal demands. The autism brain is better able to organize, retrieve, and use language to communicate when visual supports are linked to everyday activities. Parents and children make the shift from powerless to capable when a visual system is in place.

There are many excellent resources available to help you become more familiar with visual communication supports. New resources are constantly being developed around the world, including dedicated apps for use with smart (electronic) devices.

Here are some dimensions to consider when recommending the use of visual schedules to families:

- Help the parents decide on the type of visual supports that best fit their child's age and ability level. Schedules can range from the use of representational objects, photos, line drawings, to written words. Electronic systems can be used with dedicated apps for communication schedules, visual timers, and "first/then" sequences.
- Introduce types of schedules. For example, a daily schedule depicting each transition during the child's day provides predictability and organization but the child may not be ready to manage seeing all of the transitions at one time. "First/then" visual supports create mini-schedules and are effective ways to teach flexibility and communication. To help children develop a sense of anticipation regarding upcoming transitions, pairing the use of the "first/then" visual schedule with a visual timer can be helpful.
- Include an interactive component. Visual schedules are most effective when the child interacts with the schedule during transition and communication times. Taking the visual communication card off of a schedule, matching the card with an identical card placed in the area where the activity will occur, checking an event off of a list, or tapping a visual icon on a smart device are all ways a child interacts with a visual schedule to communicate his or her wants and needs. Visual

schedules are most effective when they are portable and readily available for reference during transition times throughout the child's day.
- Be prepared to provide resources for parents to learn more about creating visual schedules.

Step-by-Step Visual Maps

Think of step-by-step visual maps as a type of visual schedule. When parents of children with autism spectrum differences teach self-care and other daily routines that require a sequence of behaviors they often have to prompt the child to complete each step in the routine. Visual maps create a visual way for the child to predict and anticipate the steps in the routine. The increase in predictability reduces the child's resistance to completing the steps in the routine, as following the step-by-step visual map or schedule becomes an integral part of the routine. Visual maps support the shift from prompt-dependency to autonomy as parents are able to shift from verbal prompting to prompting the child to follow the steps outlined in the visual routine.

- Common routines that lend themselves to the use of visual step-by-step maps included getting out of bed in the morning, dressing, brushing teeth, putting things away, and doing homework.
- Include a visual depiction of the child's preferred activity at the end of the visual map or sequence to visually set up the "first/then" routine.
- As is the case with visual communication schedules, the step-by-step maps work best if the child has to perform an action on the map. Moving a card as the step depicted on the card is completed or checking boxes next to each step depicted on a chart are ways to include a dynamic and interactive component to the map process.

Organizational Systems

Children with autism spectrum brain style differences organize visually. They depend on visual structure in their surroundings to help them organize their behavior, anticipate events, and predict routines. Visually organizing the child's environment adds much needed predictability. When homework takes place in a designated area, and when visual supports in the form of organized systems list the tasks to be completed and where materials should be stored, the child with autism spectrum differences is able to visually understand the scope of the demands. When playing with toys includes a visual routine of placing objects into containers and containers in designated places, predictability becomes part of the child's routine.

- As visual organizational systems are put into place, the increase in predictability and the use of systematic routines builds cognitive flexibility and supports the shift in the family from dysregulated to controlled.

- Organizing tasks so the child experiences repeated cycles of work/break/work/break is vital to the development of cognitive flexibility. When children with autism spectrum brain style differences come into repeated contact with the routine of work/break/work/break, their resistance to work demands decreases. The experience of work demands consistently followed by breaks increases the child's ability to focus on tasks and tolerate demands.
- For young children, support parents in their use of organizational systems at home, including designating areas in the home for specific activities and visually labeling areas with pictures that can be matched using the child's visual schedule.
- For school-aged children, visual organizational supports, such as graphic organizers, are a natural fit with the autism brain style of visual, systematic, categorical thinking.
- For adolescents, visual organizational supports include the use of a notebook or binder with coaching and training on how to use the organizational binder to store school papers, materials, visual checklists, and schedules.

Resources

The following is an annotated list of resources to explore to learn more about visual schedules, step-by-step visual maps, and organizational systems:

Websites

- www.do2learn.com provides excellent visual examples of visual schedules, task sequences, "first/then" cards, and story strips.
- www.teacch.com provides excellent information about their visual approach to teaching individuals with autism spectrum differences, including detailed instructions for setting up visual schedules.
- www.iidc.indiana.edu provides excellent examples of visual schedules and communication supports through their Resource Center for Autism page.
- www.usevisualstrategies.com provides practical information about visual supports.
- www.mayer-johnson.com produces line drawings with written captions and other materials to use when developing visual schedules and communication supports.
- www.pics4learning.com provides a free image library.
- www.autismspeaks.org provides a comprehensive list of autism related apps.

- www.buildingblox.net provides excellent examples of how to organize developmental learning tasks.
- www.inspiration.com provides excellent computer-based graphic organization tools for writing and understanding concepts when reading texts.

Books

- *More Than Words* by Fern Sussman. This book provides excellent information for parents with visual graphics depicting ways to incorporate visual supports into natural conversations between parents and young children with autism spectrum differences whose language skills are emerging.
- *Visual Strategies for Improving Communication: Practical Supports for Autism Spectrum Disorders* by Linda Hodgdon. Examples of visual schedules and organizers are provided in this accessible book for parents and clinicians.
- *Visual Supports for People with Autism: A Guide for Parents and Professionals* by Marlene Cohen and Donna Sloan. This guide to visual supports includes many examples of ways to use pictures to set up visual schedules and step-by-step maps.

12 Regulation Supports

Metaphors and the Self-Regulation Scale

- Link the child's area of preferred interest to a self-regulation scale to introduce the concept of self-regulation in an accessible way.
- The creation of the scale visually supports the shift from binary thinking to incremental thinking.
- Include emotions, words, and actions into the regulation scale.

Developing Emotional Awareness and Vocabulary

- Use visual supports to teach and expand the individual's emotional awareness and vocabulary.
- Use the concept of brain training to teach flexibility and regulation.
- Help the individual and the family set a goal to practice regulation with a lower ceiling than the top level.

Understanding the Role of Sensory Regrouping Breaks

- Provide a range of sensory toys and materials during therapy sessions.
- Incorporate an action plan into the individual's regulation scale.
- Support the development of a vocabulary to communicate when the individual's sensory threshold is breached.

Metaphors and the Self-Regulation Scale

A key therapy tool for clinicians working with individuals with autism brain style differences and their families is the self-regulation scale. Discussing emotional reactivity with a visual scale as the focal point serves the function of externalizing the problem. The use of a metaphor anchors the discussion in a system that is a natural fit for the autism brain thinking style. Emotional reactivity in individuals with autism spectrum brain style differences is oftentimes experienced as a binary event as the individual moves from the "thinking" part of the brain to the "reacting" part. The creation of the self-regulation scale visually supports the shift from binary thinking to the ability to recognize increments in between two extremes. As the individual with autism spectrum differences participates in the creation of a self-regulation scale that includes the identification of emotions, words, and actions within the context of a metaphor that resonates with his or her worldview, that individual experiences the narrative shifts to capable and controlled. The process of creating a self-regulation scale may take multiple sessions. Remember to apply the "work/break/work/break" cycle during your sessions when you are requiring the individual with autism spectrum brain style differences to engage in the challenging and difficult work that goes into thinking and talking about emotions.

When you work with an individual to create a self-regulation scale, include the following steps:

- Learn about the individual's areas of interest so you can help with the selection of a metaphor that can be used as the cornerstone for the scale. Common metaphors include weather (from calm to F-5 tornado) speed (rpms from green to red), battery levels (full to empty), and thermometers.
- Create a visual scale, using three to five points on the scale. I find that scales that have five points, including the binary extreme points, are helpful in coaching individuals to expand their awareness of emotional and behavioral increments. When language abilities are less developed, a three-point scale works well.
- Start with the two extreme ends of the scale and fill in the middle progression. Support the individual in identifying the words to describe the emotions experienced at each level, the words he or she uses when at each level, and the actions he or she engages in when at each level.

Developing Emotional Awareness and Vocabulary

Regulation of emotions is a daily challenge for many individuals with autism spectrum brain style differences. The development of the individual's self-regulation scale is one tool to help build emotional awareness, vocabulary, and resilience. Familiarizing yourself with additional visual tools to include in your therapy work will equip you for the many times families ask for your help in teaching their child, adolescent, or young adult to regulate his or her emotions and behavior. Suggested resources are included at the end of this chapter.

A barrier for individuals with autism spectrum differences is the difficulty and sense of powerlessness they experience when flexibility and emotional regulation skills are required to successful manage in social settings. They are at risk for debilitating anxiety and depression, and the corresponding narrative of failure that attaches itself to those emotions.

- When you introduce the concept of brain training in your work with children, adolescents, and young adults, they are able to make the initial necessary shift to conceptualize their regulation struggles as an external task that can be systematically labeled, categorized, organized, and managed.
- As you support this shift to externalization of emotional reactivity, the individual and the family can begin to set goals to have everyone in the family practice applying the brain training tools. The result is a de-escalation of reactivity that can be discussed in terms of changes in frequency, duration, intensity, and peculiarity. Reactive episodes may continue to be intense but maybe not quite as intense as before. They may begin to occur less frequently. The individual may begin to display less extreme and unusual behaviors when agitated or distressed.
- The use of the brain-training framework and corresponding visual supports leads to systematic improvements in the area of regulation and control and a way to discuss incremental positive changes over time.
- As individuals and their families work with you to create individualized visual regulation tools, a growing sense of competence, regulation, and control replaces the narrative of powerlessness, dysregulation, and failure.

Understanding the Role of Sensory Regrouping Breaks

For many individuals with autism spectrum differences, managing incoming language, social, and work demands is hard work. The autism brain threshold for incoming demands is oftentimes much lower than the threshold neuro-typical individuals can manage. As you work with individuals and their families to support regulation skills, the role of sensory regrouping breaks plays an important role.

- Provide a range of sensory materials during therapy sessions with families. Sensory materials, such as magnet puzzles, spinning light-up toys, sensory stress balls with varied textures, inset puzzles, water toys, wind-up toys, dinosaur and animal-related objects, and popular gaming cards work well for many children with autism spectrum brain style differences. It can be helpful to have multiples of objects that can be sorted, categorized, and systematically organized. To encourage conversation about emotions, having visual prompts such as cards depicting feelings can be helpful. Noisemakers, including the percussion "thunder tube" and cause-and-effect buttons that create sounds, provide auditory input opportunities that either attract the child or are a source of anxiety. Balls, in the form of expanding spheres, balls that switch configuration when thrown, and Velcro balls with mitts provide sensory materials that can be used to create social play opportunities. The availability of sensory objects extends the child's ability to tolerate and manage the verbal aspects of the therapy sessions.

- Incorporate an action plan that includes planned, systematic sensory regrouping breaks into the individual's development of his or her regulation scale. The action plan works best if it includes a list of sensory routines that serve the function of self-regulation. The metaphors of recharging a battery or rebooting the brain system are powerful ones and work well for many individuals.
- In addition to creating a list of routines, create a list of places where the individual will go to engage in the routines.
- Help the individual identify verbal routines he or she can use to communicate when the sensory threshold has been breached. Visually place the verbal routines or phrases on the regulation scale. Consider using T-charts with the columns of "used to" and "now I" headings. List the adaptive and acceptable words and actions to use when the individual becomes agitated or distressed in the "now I" column.
- Encourage the individual to proactively engage in sensory regrouping breaks before the top level on the individual's regulation scale is reached.
- Coach the individual and the family to set up and practice the use of short, frequent, sensory regrouping breaks instead of infrequent and sustained breaks. Remember that the cycle of work/break/work/break builds flexibility and resilience.

Resources

The following is an annotated list of resources to explore to learn more about regulation supports:

Websites

- www.socialthinking.com provides excellent information on social thinking and emotional regulation materials developed by Michelle Garcia Winner for use with children with autism spectrum brain style differences.
- www.do2learn.com provides excellent visual examples of visual emotion color charts and other emotional vocabulary building tools.

- www.autism.org.uk provides excellent information and examples of visual social scripts and comic strip conversations.
- www.thetransporters.com is a computer-based program to teach emotional vocabulary and recognition of emotions with human faces attached to trains. It provides a compelling way for children who have a passionate interest in transportation to learn to recognize emotions.

Books

- *The CAT-Kit: The New Cognitive Affective Training Program for Improving Communication* by Tony Attwood, Kirsten Callesen, and Annette Moller Nielsen. This workbook-style book provides visual materials to use in teaching children and adolescents emotional vocabulary and regulation strategies.
- *The Incredible 5-Point Scale: Assisting Students with Autism Spectrum Disorders in Understanding Social Interactions and Controlling Their Emotional Responses* by Kari Dunn. Multiple examples of 5-point scales are the focus of this book.
- *Superflex . . . A Superhero Social Thinking Curriculum Package* by Stephanie Madrigal and Michelle Garcia Winner. Cartoon superheroes are used to teach emotional regulation and social skills.
- *My Mouth Is a Volcano!* by Julia Cook. This book and the rest of her series provide excellent story books that target emotional regulation tools and social thinking skills.

13 Social Narrative Supports

Developing the Self-Determination Narrative

- Create the individual's Brain Style Profile, starting with strengths and including differences.
- Compile a book about the individual, adding content across sessions.
- Tailor the format to the age and developmental level of the child or adolescent.

Building Social Awareness with the Cultural Anthropologist Metaphor

- Observing and reporting on the behavior of others;
- Gathering facts and information;
- Documenting and applying social information.

Practicing Social Skills

- Create routines within the therapy conversation to teach flexibility and shared social exchanges.
- Use visual supports to expand the individual's awareness of the perspective of others.
- Develop self-advocacy tools.

Developing the Self-Determination Narrative

A central narrative in the therapy process when working with individuals with autism spectrum differences and their families involves telling that person's singular story. For many families, the development of the individual's Brain Style Profile, organized in the three key areas of language and communication, social relationships and emotions, and sensory use and interests is the starting point. The development of the individual's Brain Style Profile is the first of many documents that work together to form a tangible way to think and talk about the child, adolescent, or young adult's strengths, abilities, talents, and differences. Encouraging families to create a book about the individual provides a structured way to add information and content across sessions. The format of the book can be tailored to match the age and developmental level of the child or adolescent.

- Use the language provided in the Descriptive Triangle to create the individual's Brain Style Profile. Identify areas of strength and then areas of difference across the three key areas of: language and communication, social relationships and emotions, and sensory use and interests.
- Include basic strategies and resources to support the development of skills in each of the three key areas. For example, listing the reminder to "show while telling" under language and communication reminds parents of young children to adapt their communication style. It reminds older children and adolescents to recognize what they need and what situations are likely to trigger anxiety, agitation, withdrawal, or distress.
- Encourage the development of a personal narrative book, providing a reference and resource where individual's narrative documents are stored. Promote the idea of having the individual select the notebook and decorate it to personalize the book. When the child or adolescent places images of beloved topics on the notebook, the contents of the notebook become visually associated with his or her area of preferred interests: a positive association. The personal narrative book provides a natural way to prompt conversation during sessions, as documents are reviewed and new ones are added.
- Over the course of multiple sessions, develop a list detailing key information about the child's interests, learning style, and areas where others need to understand their unique worldview. The format of asking children and their parents to identify "3 things" establishes a routine for collecting facts and information related to the child's interest, style, and personal story.
- Here are some examples of "3 things" that can be prompted and collected:
  - I do really well;
  - About my areas of interest;

- ○   Facts about the way I learn best;
- ○   About my family;
- ○   About my pets;
- ○   I need help with from an adult who knows me;
- ○   That calm me down when I get upset;
- ○   That upset me;
- ○   I enjoy doing outside of school.

- For young children and for children and adolescents who have limited verbal fluency, the development of photo books that include simple, first-person narrative captions is a powerful way to build a singular personal narrative. The use of photo books with captions uses the natural entry point of visual details to expand the individual's awareness of and vocabulary for describing his or her social world.

Practicing Social Skills

Within the context of your sessions with families, you can create opportunities to support practicing social skills. Using modeling and coaching, the individual with autism spectrum differences and his or her parents can experience success in their ability to engage in more extensive and substantive conversations. Visual supports play an important role in supporting effective shared conversational exchanges, as they help the individuals with autism spectrum differences expand their awareness of the perspective of the conversational partner. As you create documents about the individual's brain style during sessions, you support the development of self-advocacy. The development of documents listing behaviors, words, and actions provides the individual with the necessary tools to visually review and practice those skills outside of the therapy setting.

- During therapy conversations, opportunities readily arise to help the child or adolescent practice social conversational skills. Many individuals with autism spectrum differences initiate or start conversations but struggle to include or respond to their conversational partner. Using the metaphor of "train your brain," you can coach the individual to practice flexibility and shared exchanges.
- To increase the individual's ability to participate in a shared social exchange, set up a brief (two or three exchanges) routine using a ball and a conversational partner. You can model this with the child and then coach the parents to use the "talk" ball. The use of a tangible object that serves as a signifier or placeholder provides the visual dimension necessary to highlight when to talk and when to listen. As you shape the use of the "talk ball" to extend shared communication between the child and his or her parents, keep in mind that the exchange is most successful when the required listening time is brief

and the child is only expected to practice two or three exchanges at a time. You may notice that when you introduce this routine the child will naturally create a sensory regrouping break in between conversational demands by retreating to manipulate your sensory toys and materials before returning to engage in the hard work of managing a social conversation.

- The use of a tangible "pause" button is another useful visual tool to teach the individual to "train my brain" to shift back and forth between the autism agenda and the social one.
- A key document in helping children, adolescents, and young adults develop self-advocacy skills involves the creation of a list of "5 things my teacher needs to know about me," or "5 things my employer needs to know about me," or "5 things my friends need to know about me." These lists are most powerful when the first two items on the list identify areas of strength, progressing down the list to areas of difference that require understanding and additional supports.

Building Social Awareness with the Cultural Anthropologist Metaphor

As you become skilled in developing Brain Style Profiles with children, adolescents, and young adults with autism spectrum differences you will notice some key learning styles emerge. The terms "visual thinker," "systematic thinker," "binary thinker," and "scientific thinker" are descriptive of many individuals with the autism spectrum brain style. Gathering facts and information, placing information into categories or systems, and storing information in a visual way represent brain style strengths that can be applied to the task of building social awareness. For individuals who categorize information related to their areas of preferred interest but who struggle to recognize and use social cues, the metaphor of the cultural anthropologist can be powerful.

- Introduce the metaphor of becoming a cultural anthropologist by discussing the goal of having the child enter a social situation with the goal of observing the behavior of others. The goal of the cultural observation is to collect facts and information to place into classifications and categories that will aid in the understanding of the function of the behavior routines. This goal of observing and reporting provides the necessary framework to allow the child to enter into a social situation in a goal-directed way. They have a role and an assignment. This structure provides the gateway for the individual with autism spectrum differences to build social awareness.
- As the child is given the goal-directed task of observing and reporting, valuable information emerges regarding the focal point of the child's observations. This information informs the necessary

coaching to expand the child's ability to gather facts and information about social details. Goals can then be set to expand the child's focus when observing, reporting, and gathering facts and information.

- As part of the social facts and information gathering, the child can collect specific information. For example, starting a list of: "classmates I want to get to know better" can lead to a fact-finding social excursion, where the child gathers the following type of information:
  - three facts about the person I learned from asking questions;
  - three facts I will tell the person about myself;
  - three activities I would consider asking this person to do with me.
- The information gathered during the cultural anthropology excursions can be added to the child's self-determination notebook. The inclusion of this collected information supports the child's ability to apply the social information in daily life.

Resources

The following is an annotated list of resources to explore to learn more about social narrative supports:

Websites

- www.autism.org.uk provides excellent information and examples of visual social scripts and comic strip conversations.
- www.modelmekids.com provides excellent examples of how to develop photo narratives.
- www.coultervideo.com provides several excellent DVDs and downloads for adolescents and young adults with high-functioning autism spectrum differences. The DVD *Manners for the Real World: Social Skills* features a young man with spectrum differences as the guide to the content.
- www.robokindrobots.com, specifically the page Robots4Autism, introduces the technology of Milo, the humanoid-featured robot designed to teach social skills to children with autism spectrum brain style differences.

Books

- *The Social Skills Picture Book Teaching Play, Emotion, and Communication to Children with Autism* by Jed Baker. This excellent book provides photographs and social scripts covering a range of social and emotional situations. His companion book for adolescents is also a good resource (*The Social Skills Picture Book for High School and Beyond*).

- *The New Social Story Book* by Carol Gray. This book contains pre-written social stories about many common life events, using a specific style and structure developed by the author.
- *You Are a Social Detective* by Michelle Garcia Winner. This illustrated book for children applies the social detective metaphor to teach social awareness skills. She has multiple books in her series on social thinking.

A Final Conversation

This brings us to the end of our autism conversations in narrative practice. Over the arc of this book you have accompanied a number of individuals and their families as they applied descriptive language and a visual framework to better understand what autism means. Techniques were modeled that supported the narrative shifts from powerlessness, dysregulation, prompt-dependence, and disorder to the empowering narratives of competence, regulation, autonomy, and style. The distinctive challenges facing families over the arc of the life cycle, from early childhood to young adulthood, were shown, as individuals and their families worked on their narratives in the therapy setting.

The work you do with individuals with autism spectrum brain style differences and their families makes a difference. Thank you for sharing the autism conversations in this book. Apply the ideas presented here in your clinical practice, and may you continue to have many substantive, respectful, and helpful autism conversations.

Change the story, and you change the life.

Index

Note: Page numbers with *f*, *t*, and *b* indicate figures, tables, and boxes respectively.